Silver Burdett & Ginn
SCIENCE

GEORGE G. MALLINSON
Distinguished Professor
of Science Education
Western Michigan University

JACQUELINE B. MALLINSON
Associate Professor of Science
Western Michigan University

WILLIAM L. SMALLWOOD
Head, Science Department
The Community School
Sun Valley, Idaho

CATHERINE VALENTINO
Former Director of Instruction
North Kingstown School Department
North Kingstown, Rhode Island

SILVER BURDETT & GINN
LEXINGTON, MA • MORRISTOWN, NJ
Atlanta, GA • Cincinnati, OH • Dallas, TX • Menlo Park, CA • Northfield, IL

THE SILVER BURDETT & GINN
ELEMENTARY SCIENCE PROGRAM

Pupil Books Levels 1-6
Teacher Editions Levels K-6

Silver Burdett & Ginn
SCIENCE

Contents

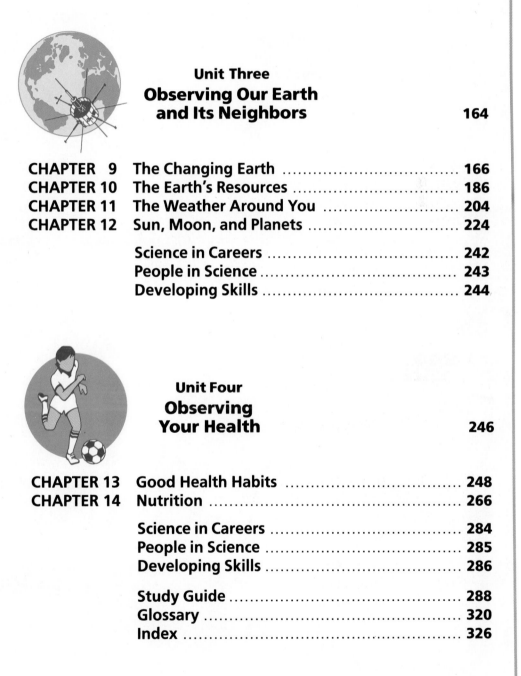

Unit Three
Observing Our Earth and Its Neighbors
164

Unit Four
Observing Your Health
246

The Adventure of Science

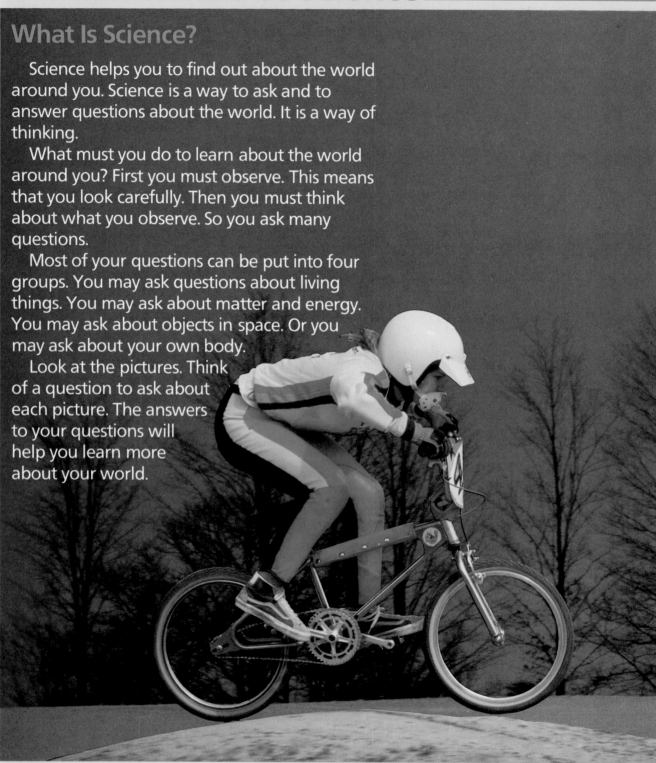

What Is Science?

Science helps you to find out about the world around you. Science is a way to ask and to answer questions about the world. It is a way of thinking.

What must you do to learn about the world around you? First you must observe. This means that you look carefully. Then you must think about what you observe. So you ask many questions.

Most of your questions can be put into four groups. You may ask questions about living things. You may ask about matter and energy. You may ask about objects in space. Or you may ask about your own body.

Look at the pictures. Think of a question to ask about each picture. The answers to your questions will help you learn more about your world.

A

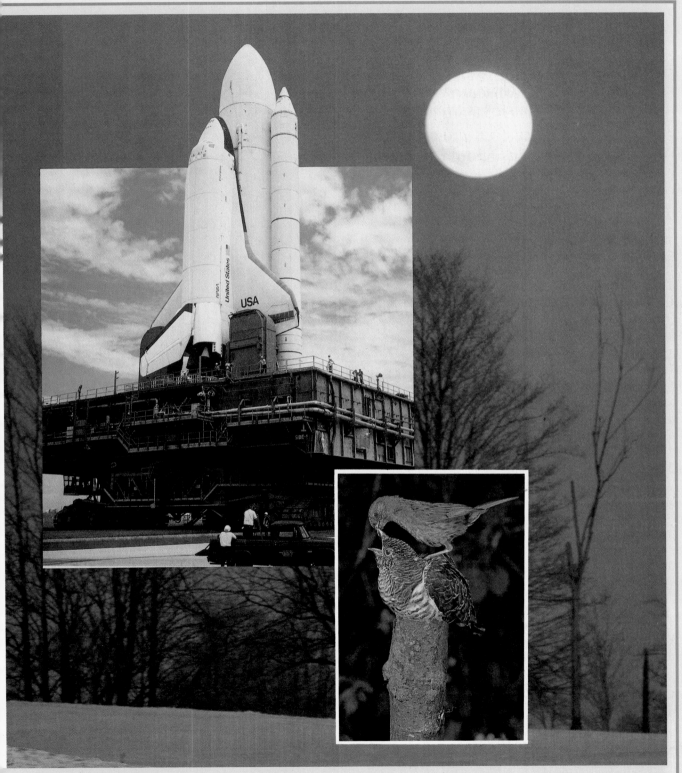

What Will You Learn in Science?

In science class you will learn how to think about things. You will learn how to solve problems. You will also learn how to be a good observer. In science class you can find the answers to questions about the world.

Look at the children in the picture. They are doing a science activity. What do you think they are trying to find out? What questions do you think these children are asking?

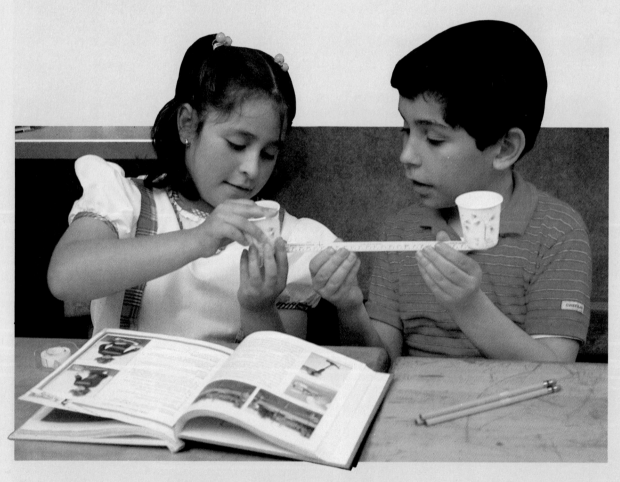

How Is Science Important to Me?

Think about what is happening in each of these pictures. In what season of the year does ice form on a pond? How are these children making bubbles? What do the boy and girl know about living things? Why is this boy washing his knee? What might happen if he did not wash it?

Hold Everything

How do scientists solve problems? Scientists work to help people. They try to help people understand things that happen in the world. Scientists also help people to solve problems. One problem people have is finding the right containers to hold different kinds of matter.

What kinds of containers do people use? Look around your classroom. Make a list of all the containers you see. How many did you find? How are they different from each other? What problem does each one solve?

Draw a picture of a new kind of container. What problem does your container solve?

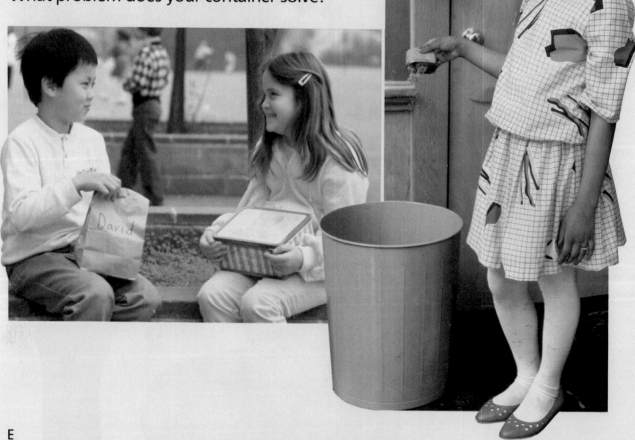

Koko's Kitten

You have learned what science is. And you have learned how scientists solve problems. Now read about a special animal named Koko.

Koko is a gorilla. She is about 14 years old. Dr. Patterson is a scientist. She wanted to find out how animals learn. So she studied Koko.

Scientists have taught Koko to use her hands to make signs. Each sign is for a different word. Koko uses the signs to name things.

Dr. Patterson keeps a record of what Koko does. Why is it helpful to keep records?

One day someone gave Dr. Patterson three kittens. Dr. Patterson showed the kittens to Koko. Koko looked at the kittens. She made signs that said *love that.* Then Koko made a sign that said *cat.*

Koko looked at each kitten very carefully. Then she picked a kitten that had no tail. Koko made signs for the kitten's name. She made signs that said *all ball.* How did the scientist know that All Ball was to be the kitten's name?

Dr. Patterson wondered if Koko would like to have All Ball for a pet. She handed the kitten to Koko gently. Dr. Patterson had to be sure that Koko would not hurt the kitten. Koko took the kitten. Then Koko made signs that said *soft good cat cat.*

Dr. Patterson watched the two animals together. She knew that All Ball would be a good pet for Koko. How do you think Dr. Patterson knew this?

H

All Ball was a very playful and frisky kitten. He liked to run and jump on Koko. Sometimes All Ball would even bite Koko on the leg. But Koko would never hurt the kitten. Sometimes Koko would wrap All Ball in a napkin. At other times she would rock the kitten back and forth.

Koko liked to be tickled. Dr. Patterson watched Koko make the sign that said *tickle* to All Ball. Then Koko would try to tickle All Ball. Koko was showing All Ball what to do.

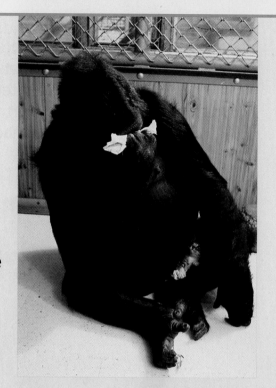

One day a sad thing happened. All Ball was hit by a car. Dr. Patterson made signs to tell Koko that she would never see her kitten again. Koko seemed sad. She did not want to play. The scientists knew that losing All Ball caused Koko to act this way. How could the scientists test this idea?

Dr. Patterson brought Koko another kitten. The new kitten was orange. When Dr. Patterson asked Koko what the new kitten's name was, Koko made the sign for *lipstick.* The new kitten had a very pink nose. Perhaps the nose looked like a person's pink lips. Later Koko would call the kitten Lips.

What do you think scientists can learn from studying the behavior of an animal? Why do you think Koko was a good animal for scientists to study?

Unit One

Observing Plants and Animals

Chapter 1—Animals Animals care for their young in different ways. A penguin (pen'gwin) chick rides on its parent's feet. There the chick is fed and protected.

Chapter 3— Seed Plants Have you ever seen a sunflower? Seeds form in this flower. The seeds are produced so that new plants can grow.

Chapter 2–Animals Are Important

Animals like the sea otter must be protected from harm. In this chapter you will find out what can happen when animals are not protected.

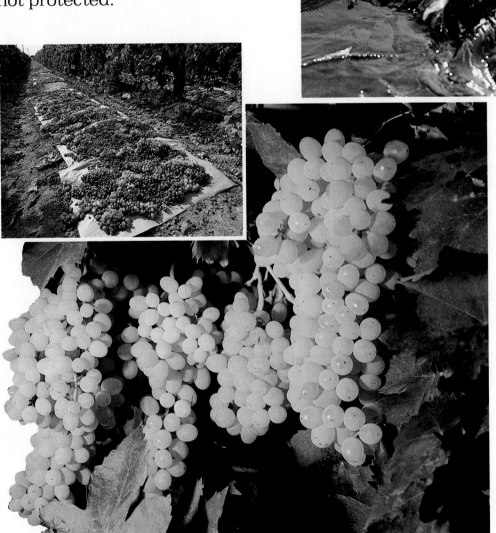

Chapter 4–Plants Are Important
Raisins are made from grapes that are dried in the sun. In this chapter you will learn about other uses of plants.

Chapter 1

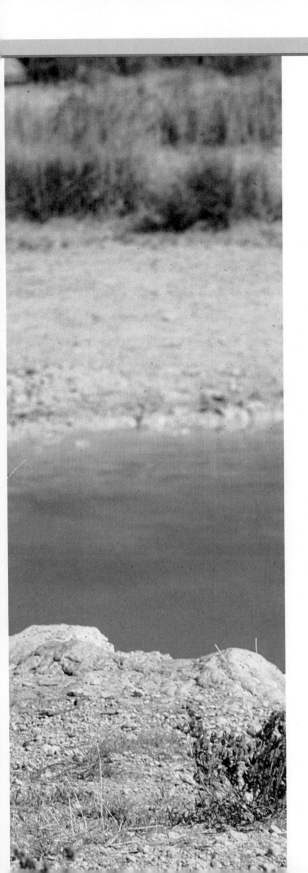

Animals

There are many kinds of animals. Some live on land. Others live in water. Most animals move around. Some walk, some crawl, some fly, and some swim. A few hardly move at all.

What kinds of animals did you see today? Were they all the same size? The same age? Did you see any animals with their young?

All animals produce more of their own kind. What would happen if they did not? In this chapter you will learn about animals and their young. You will find out how the young grow and change.

Animals and Their Young

How do animals produce young?

You probably have seen chicken eggs many times. But have you ever seen turtle eggs? Or the eggs of a grasshopper? Turtles, grasshoppers, and many other animals lay eggs. What animals do you know that lay eggs?

grasshopper

fish

bird

snake

toad

Snapping turtle laying an egg

Most animals come from eggs. The eggs are produced by the female animals. The number of eggs produced by each kind of animal is different. Some birds lay only one egg a year, but most birds lay several.

4

Another animal, the toad, lays up to 6,000 eggs at a time. An oyster (ois'tər), however, may lay as many as 500 million eggs at a time.

Many eggs contain everything needed to form a new animal. Look closely at these frog eggs. Can you see the new animal forming in each egg?

Frog eggs

1

2

3

Many eggs have a shell or other covering. The covering keeps the egg from drying out. It also protects the new animal growing inside. Bird eggs have a hard shell. Turtle eggs have a softer shell that is like leather. Frog and snail eggs have a jellylike covering.

When the animal has grown enough, it breaks out of the egg. This is called hatching. Here you can see how a chicken hatches.

Western garter snake and young

Some animals do not lay eggs. Instead, the eggs hatch inside the female's body. After hatching, the live young pass out of her body. Guppies (gup'ēz), most sharks, and some snakes produce young this way.

Other animals also give birth to living young. But these young do not hatch from eggs. They grow in a special way in the female's body. When the young are born, the mother produces milk to feed them. Cows, dogs, and most other mammals (mam'əls) produce young this way. A **mammal** is an animal that has hair and feeds its young with mother's milk.

Cow and newborn calf

Mother pigs feeding young

What are the parts of a chicken egg?

Materials hand lens / cold hard-cooked egg / uncooked egg / dish / dinner knife

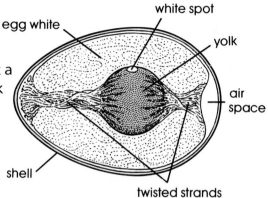

Procedure

A. Tap both ends of a hard-cooked egg against a hard surface. Carefully peel away the shell. Look for an air space at one of the ends of the egg. Find the thin lining inside the shell. Examine a piece of the shell, using a hand lens.

   1. Describe the shell.

B. Cut open the hard-cooked egg. Examine it closely.

   2. Describe what you see.

C. Carefully break an uncooked egg into a dish. Compare the egg to the drawing.

   3. Point to the parts of the egg you can identify.

D. Find the twisted strands of egg white.

   4. What do you think would happen if the strands broke?

E. Identify the white spot on the yolk. This is the spot where a baby chicken would begin to grow.

   5. Where would the baby chicken get its food?

F. Compare the egg white to the egg yolk.

   6. Describe how they are different.

Conclusion

1. What parts of the chicken egg did you see?
2. How is each part of the egg important for the new animal that may grow inside it?

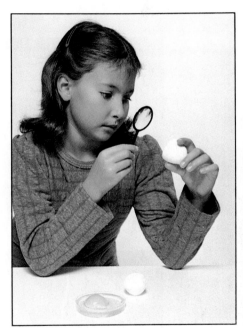

7

Animals Grow and Change

How do certain animals change as they grow?

Many young animals look much like their parents. Others do not. Some go through stages of growth. In each stage of growth they become more like their parents. Look at the pictures below. Notice how the frog changes in each stage of growth. How does the adult frog differ from the young frog in the first picture? How are they the same?

1

2

3

4

Insects also change as they grow. Many go through four stages of growth. Those stages are (1) egg, (2) larva (lär′və), (3) pupa (pyü′pə), and (4) adult. Some insects that change this way are butterflies, moths, and beetles.

Butterfly eggs hatching

The **egg** is the first stage of growth. Insect eggs may be laid almost anywhere. Often they are on leaves or other food the insects can eat after they hatch.

After hatching, the young insect is called a **larva.** A larva is in the second stage of growth. A larva is always hungry. This larva is eating a leaf.

Gypsy moth pupa

Moth larva

After a certain time, a larva stops eating. Then it makes a covering for itself. The covering is usually hard. Now the insect is called a **pupa.** A pupa is in the third stage of growth.

9

Monarch butterfly

Inside the covering, the pupa slowly changes. When the changes are complete, the **adult** insect comes out. This is the fourth stage of growth. Now the insect looks the same as other adults of its kind.

The butterfly in the picture is a new adult. Only a few moments earlier it was a pupa. The butterfly is resting on the covering that it had as a pupa. When its wings are dry, the butterfly will fly away.

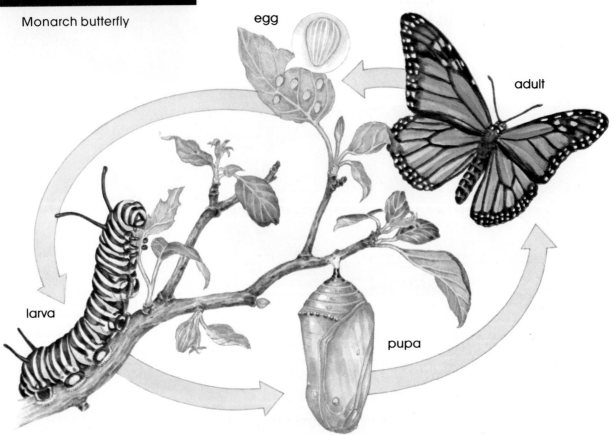

egg

adult

larva

pupa

BUTTERFLY STAGES OF GROWTH

Grasshopper nymph

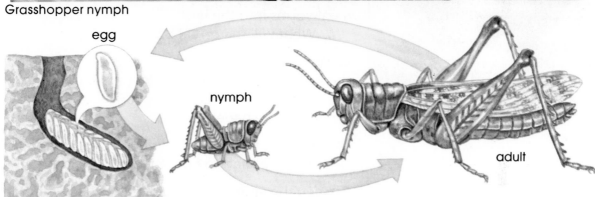
egg

nymph

adult

GRASSHOPPER STAGES OF GROWTH

Some insects, such as grasshoppers, have only three stages of growth. They are (1) egg, (2) nymph (nimf), and (3) adult. After hatching, the young insect is called a **nymph.** A nymph is like a tiny adult. But it does not have wings. The nymph becomes an adult insect when it has wings and can fly.

How does a mealworm change as it grows?

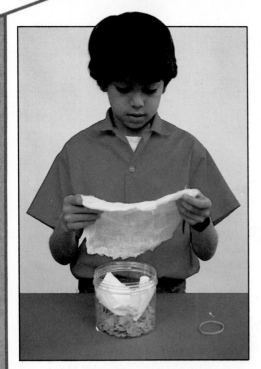

Materials   jar / dry cereal / 5 to 10 mealworms / paper towels / piece of cloth / rubber band

Procedure

A. Mealworms are the larva of insects called grain beetles. Put 5 to 10 mealworms on a paper towel. Watch them for a few minutes.
   1. What does a mealworm look like?
   2. How does a mealworm move?
   3. What do you think a mealworm must have to live?

B. Half fill a jar with dry cereal. Then put the mealworms into the jar.
   4. What will the cereal be used for?

C. Wet a paper towel, and squeeze out most of the water. Lay the towel on the cereal in the jar.
   5. What do you think the mealworms will get from the paper towel?

D. Cover the top of the jar with a piece of cloth. Use a rubber band to hold the cloth in place.

E. Keep the jar in a warm, dry place. Clean the jar every few days. Each time, give the mealworms fresh cereal and a new, wet paper towel.

F. Watch for changes that take place as the mealworms grow. Describe what you see in a chart like the one shown. Describe how the animals look and act each time you watch them.

Date	Stage	Description

Conclusion

1. Was there a stage of growth that you did not see? Which one?

2. In what ways does a mealworm change during each stage of growth?

Caring for the Young

How do animal parents care for their young?

Some young animals can take care of themselves right away. They do not need parents to help them. Most fish are on their own as soon as they hatch. Newly hatched turtles can walk and eat like adults.

Science & Technology

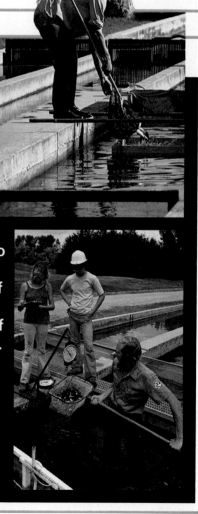

▶ Fish farming is a way of raising more fish for people to eat. Sometimes young fish are raised in holding tanks. There the farmers can control the temperature of the water. They can also control the food the fish eat.

▶ Young fish that are kept in tanks are protected from harm. When these fish grow to a certain size, they are put into larger bodies of water.

◀ Catfish are one kind of fish raised on fish farms. At harvest time, large numbers of catfish are pulled from the water. Think of some reasons why fish farming is becoming very important.

Robin feeding young

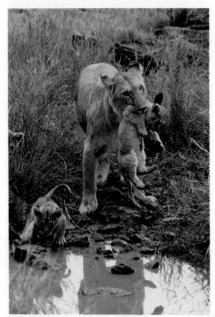

Lioness carrying her cub

Other young animals cannot live on their own. They must be cared for by one or both parents. Most birds are like that. These robins would die if they were not fed. Why? How else must they be cared for?

Mammals also need care after they are born. What is the special way all mammals are cared for?

Many newborn mammals are helpless. Some, such as bear cubs, are born blind and without hair. Some, such as puppies and kittens, cannot stand up by themselves. But a deer or a bison (bīs'ən) is different. It can see right away. It can stand up within minutes after it is born. After about an hour, it can follow its mother wherever she goes.

Bison with newborn calf

Dog feeding puppies

Finding Out

Which animals, other than kangaroos, are marsupials?

Kangaroos belong to an unusual group of mammals called marsupials (mär sü'pē əlz). Marsupials carry their young in a pouch until they are quite big. While in the pouch, the young kangaroo is fed by its mother.

But the kangaroo is not the only kind of marsupial. Look in books about animals to find the names of some other kinds of marsupials.

Young mammals need more than food. They must be protected from animals that can harm them. Also, some mammals need special skills to live on their own. The young learn those skills by watching their parents. What skill are these bear cubs learning?

Alaskan brown bear with cubs

Mammals need less care as they grow older and stronger. These lion cubs are hunting their own food. Soon they will be able to live on their own. They will not need to be cared for by their parents.

Lion cubs hunting

Ideas to Remember

▶ Most animals come from eggs.

▶ Some animals produce young from eggs hatched inside the female's body.

▶ Most mammals give birth to living young.

▶ Many insects go through four stages of growth—egg, larva, pupa, and adult.

▶ Some young animals can live on their own. Others must be cared for by parents.

Reviewing the Chapter

A. Use all the terms below to fill in the blanks.

pupa   egg   adult   nymph   larva

Some young animals look much like their parents. Others do not. Many insects go through four stages of growth before they look like their parents. The first stage is the __1__. After hatching, the young insect is called a __2__. Later, the young insect makes a covering for itself. Now it is called a __3__. Changes take place inside the covering. When the changes are complete, the __4__ insect comes out. Some insects, such as the grasshopper, have only three stages of growth. They are the egg, the __5__, and the adult stages.

B. Unscramble each group of letters to find a science term from the chapter. Write a sentence using each term.

1. cisnet   **2.** mlmama   **3.** thcah

A. The drawings show the stages of growth of a moth. Write the numbers of the drawings to show the correct order.

B. Some animals have many young. Others have very few. Which animals do you think would give the best care to their young? Give reasons for your answers.

C. Write the letter of the animal that best matches each statement.

1. Its eggs hatch inside the female's body.
2. It lays hard-shelled eggs.
3. It lays jellylike eggs.
4. It has three growth stages.
5. It has hair and gets milk from its mother.

   a. grasshopper
   b. mammal
   c. bird
   d. guppy
   e. frog

USING IDEAS

Walk around your neighborhood. List the animals you see. Which of those animals lay eggs? Which give birth to live young?

THINKING LIKE A SCIENTIST

You may be able to answer some of these questions just by thinking about them. To answer other questions, you may have to do some research.

1. Scientists can learn about animals by carefully gathering information about them. How do scientists know that animals grow and change?
2. Many insects do not live long enough to lay eggs. Insects are often eaten by other animals. Sometimes, changes in the weather kill many insects. During which stage of growth do you think insects are in the most danger? Give reasons for your answers.
3. Sea turtles dig their nests on a beach, away from the water. After they lay their eggs, they cover their nests with sand. Then they go back into the ocean. When the baby turtles hatch, they cannot see the ocean clearly. Still, they are able to find their way to the water. Think of three reasons why they might know which way to go.
4. Most animals are born or hatched in the spring. Think of some reasons to explain this.

Chapter 2

Animals Are Important

Which animal, do you think, is most important to people? No one can say for sure. Almost all animals are important to people in some way. People keep animals as pets. People also use many things that come from animals.

The picture shows an animal that is useful to people. Years ago, many whales like this one swam in the oceans. Today there are fewer whales. What do you think happened to the whales?

In this chapter you will learn why animals are important to people. You will also learn why some animals must be protected.

Foods from Animals

Which foods come from animals?

Many of the things you use each day come from animals. You may eat foods that come from animals. Many things you wear come from animals. Without animals, there are many things you would not have.

Milking cows

Pig farm

Shopping for meat

You probably drink milk every day. Milk is an important food that comes from cows. Milk can be used to make butter and cheese. Cattle are raised for their meat. The meat from cattle is called beef.

People eat the meat of other animals, too. The meat from a pig is called pork. Ham and bacon also come from a pig. The meat from chickens, turkeys, and ducks is also eaten.

Birds that are used for food are called **poultry** (pōl′trē). What other food comes from poultry?

Cattle, pigs, and birds are raised by people. Some other animals used for food are not raised by people. Many of these animals live in oceans, rivers, and streams. These animals are wild and must be caught.

Have you ever eaten tuna or salmon (sam′ən)? Tuna and salmon are fish. Most tuna and salmon live in the salt water of oceans. Large nets are used to catch these fish. Here you can see that many fish are caught at one time.

Collecting eggs

Ocean fishing

tuna

salmon

23

trout

bass

perch

Fishing in fresh water

Other kinds of fish are caught in the fresh water of rivers, lakes, and streams. Some of these fish are bass, trout, and perch. In some places, fish is a very important food.

Do You Know?

Honeybees are the only insects that are able to produce a food for people to eat. That food is honey. To make honey, the bees collect sweet nectar (nek′ tər) from flowers. As the nectar is collected, it is stored in a special pouch in the bee's body. Then the honeybee carries the nectar to the hive. There the nectar slowly changes from a watery liquid to a thick liquid. The flavor and color of honey depend upon the flower the nectar comes from.

People Raise Other Animals

Which useful animals do people raise?

Many useful things come from animals. Perhaps you have used some of them. Have you ever slept on a pillow stuffed with feathers? The soft feathers found in most pillows come from ducks and geese. These feathers are called **down.** Down is also used in coats and sleeping bags.

Wool is another useful thing that comes from animals. The hair of a sheep is called wool. In the picture, you can see how wool is cut from a sheep. This wool may be used to

Down-filled jacket

Sheepshearing and wool sweater

make clothing and blankets. Many things made from wool are warm and soft.

Some animal skins are also useful. The skins of cattle, sheep, and pigs are called **hides.** Most of these animal hides are used to make leather shoes and leather clothing. Belts, gloves, and footballs can also be made from leather.

Leather objects

Guide dog

If you have a pet, you know another good reason why people need animals. Dogs and cats make good pets. Name some other animals that might make good pets.

Dogs are important to people in other ways. Sometimes dogs are trained to help people who cannot see. Dogs are also trained to protect property.

There are other animals that people depend on. These are animals that can help people to do work. In some places, elephants are used to lift heavy logs. This picture shows how horses help to herd cattle. Horses have also been used to pull loads. Perhaps you can name other animals that help people in some way.

Working elephant

Herding cattle

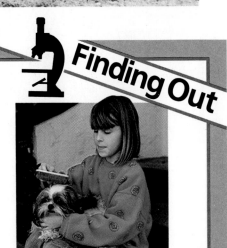
Finding Out

What are the duties of pet owners?

If you have a pet, make a list of the things you must do to take care of your pet properly. If you do not have a pet, talk to someone who does. Find out about such things as feeding, cleaning, and health care. When you have gathered this information, discuss the needs of different kinds of pets with your classmates.

Activity

Which animals do people use for food?

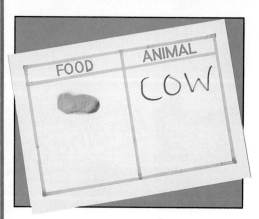

Materials newspapers and magazines / scissors / poster paper / glue

Procedure

A. Make a chart like the one shown.

B. Look in newspapers and magazines that have ads for foods or pictures of foods. Find ads for and pictures of foods that come from animals. Also look for foods that are made from animal products.

C. Cut out ads and pictures you find.

D. Paste the ads and pictures on the chart. Next to each, write the name of the animal that the food or food product came from.

Conclusion

1. Look at the animal names that you have written on the chart. How many different animal names are on the chart?

2. Which animal's name is written the most number of times?

3. Which animal's name is written the fewest number of times?

4. Which of the animals on the chart have been raised by people?

5. Which of the animals on the chart are wild animals?

Using science ideas

How might the use of animals by people cause a problem?

Endangered Animals

Why are some wild animals endangered?

Many wild animals are important for their meat, hides, and other things. This is why people have always hunted these animals.

Many whales used to swim in the oceans. They swam together in large groups. But whales were needed for their fat. This fat, called blubber (blub′ər), was used to make whale oil. The oil was burned in lamps for light. Whales were also important for their meat and bone. Because of this, people hunted and killed whales. More whales were killed than were born. Soon there were very few whales. When only a few animals of a certain kind remain, that kind of animal is **endangered** (en dān′jərd). Now whales are endangered animals.

Sea turtle

Tortoise

Like the whale, many other kinds of wild animals are endangered. Too many of them have been hunted and killed. Some turtles have been killed for their shells. The shells are used to make jewelry. Wild cats such as tigers and leopards (lep′ərdz) have been

Bengal tiger

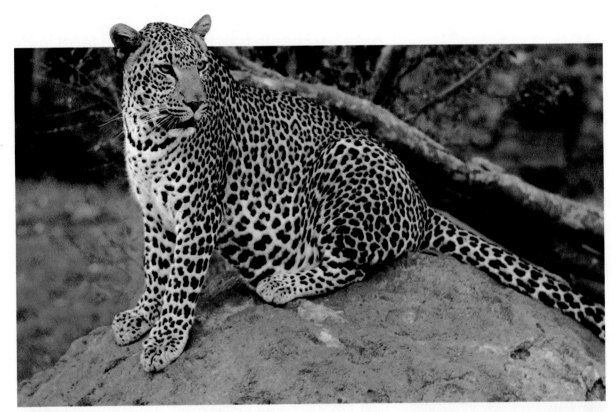

Leopard

killed for their fur. Elephants are hunted for their long white tusks. These tusks are made of ivory (ī'vər ē). Ivory is used to make beautiful things. All of these animals are now endangered.

Some wild animals are endangered for another reason. People have changed the places where these wild animals live. Because of this, the animals do not have places to raise their young.

Many of the places where elephants live have been changed. Most elephants live in grasslands. Grasslands have been changed

African elephant

because people need more land to farm and build houses. Now there are fewer places for elephants to live.

The bald eagle is also an endangered animal. People have cleared many forests where this bird builds its nests. Without places to build nests, the bald eagle cannot produce young. People sometimes use poisons to kill insect pests. The insects are eaten by fish, which are eaten by the eagles. The poisons can then harm the eagles.

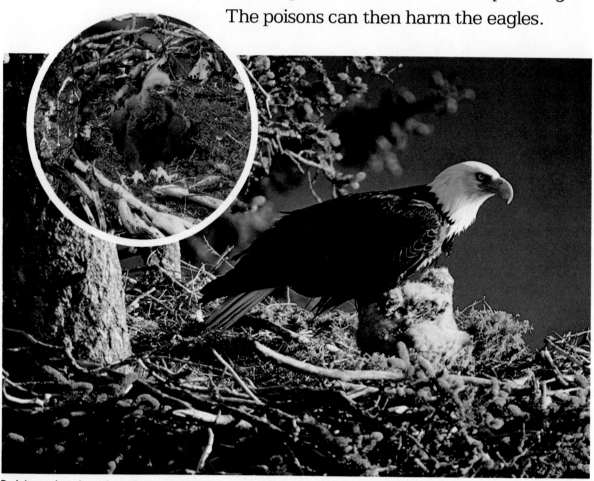

Bald eagle at nest and young eagle

Where do wild animals live?

Materials pictures of wild animals / crayons / scissors / shoebox / construction paper / glue

Procedure

A. Look at the pictures of the wild animals. Think about the many different kinds of places where wild animals live.

   1. Name each animal you see and describe the place where it lives.

B. Choose one wild animal and then draw a picture of it.

   2. Which animal did you choose?

C. Carefully cut out the picture of the wild animal you drew.

D. Use the inside of a shoebox to make a model of the place where your wild animal lives.

E. Glue the picture of the animal you drew to the model.

Conclusion

1. What kind of place did you make a model of?

2. Why is this a good place for the wild animal to live?

Using science ideas

In some places, people clear land to build houses and roads. What do you think happens to the wild animals living in these places?

33

Animals Need People

How are endangered animals protected?

Dodo bird

This animal is a dodo (dō′dō) bird. You can only see this kind of a bird in a picture. The dodo bird is extinct (ek stingkt′). An animal that is **extinct** is gone forever.

Here is a condor. There are less than 50 of these birds living. They live in a wildlife refuge (wīld′līf   ref′yüj). A **wildlife refuge** is a place where wild animals are safe. If there were no refuges, many wild animals like the condor would become extinct.

Laws have also been made to protect wild animals. These laws control hunting, fishing,

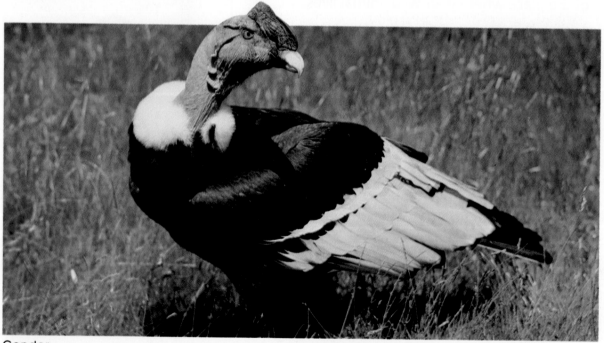

Condor

and trapping. Some kinds of wild animals may not be hunted or caught at all. Other kinds of animals may be hunted or caught only at certain times. This is to protect some kinds of animals when they are having their young. Laws like this help many endangered animals.

Safe place for eagles

Control of hunting

Ideas to Remember

▶ Many useful things come from animals.

▶ People raise some of the animals they use.

▶ Many kinds of wild animals are hunted and killed.

▶ Some kinds of wild animals are endangered.

▶ Many wild animals are being protected.

Reviewing the Chapter

A. Use all the terms below to complete the sentences.

poultry   hides   cattle   down   cows

    Many things you use each day come from animals.
You might drink milk that comes from __1__ and eat
beef that comes from __2__. The meat of chickens,
turkeys, and ducks is also eaten. Birds that are raised
to be used for food are called __3__. Other useful
things come from animals. Soft feathers from ducks
and geese are used to make pillows. These feathers
are called __4__. The skins of sheep, pigs, and cattle
are also useful. These skins are called __5__.

B. Find the missing letters for each term. Write a sentence using
each term.

1. __ n __ a n __ e __ __ d
2. e __ t __ n c __
3. w __ l __ li __ e __ e __ u __ e

UNDERSTANDING IDEAS

A. Write the letter of the term that goes with the animal. Not all
the terms will be used.

1. sheep	**a.** ivory
2. whale	**b.** fur
3. cattle	**c.** bacon
4. elephant	**d.** wool
5. pig	**e.** down
	f. beef
	g. blubber

B. Tell what would happen if the
number of adult bluebirds dying is
greater than the number born.

C. Make a chart like the one shown. Write the names of animals from the chapter under each heading.

Useful animals people raise	Wild animals people hunt	Endangered animals

Make a poster to let people know about an endangered animal.

You may be able to answer some of these questions just by thinking about them. To answer other questions, you may have to do some research.

1. Years ago, farmers used animals to help them with their work. Animals such as horses and oxen were used to pull heavy loads. Today, farmers use machines to do this work. Give some reasons why it is cheaper to use machines in place of work animals.

2. Scientists can learn about pollution by observing and studying animals. What things would a scientist want to observe?

3. Measuring and counting are very important learning tools that scientists use every day. Some scientists try to find out how many endangered animals of one kind exist in a large region. How could they find out the total number of endangered animals in a large region without counting each one?

4. Sometimes a farmer's crop fails or a herd of animals becomes ill. How can science help farmers to solve problems like these?

Seed Plants

What kinds of plants did you see today? Did any of them look like the plants in the picture? These plants appear to be very different. They have different shapes and sizes. Some are different colors. Although these plants seem to be different, they are alike. They all are seed plants. Why, do you think, are they called seed plants?

Most seed plants have the same kinds of plant parts. The parts may not always look the same in all plants, but they do the same jobs.

In this chapter you will learn about seed plants. You will learn about their roots, stems, leaves, and other parts.

Roots

What do roots do?

Have you ever tried to pull out weeds in a garden? Did they come out easily? Weeds and most other seed plants have roots that grow in the ground. In some plants, the roots may grow more than 6 meters deep. Roots hold plants in place. Look at these trees. Even a strong wind usually cannot blow them over.

What else do roots do? Roots take in the water and minerals (min'ər əls) plants need.

Palm trees in a storm

Plants need minerals to grow and to be healthy. The water and minerals are carried in tiny tubes in the roots to the stem.

In some plants, food is stored in the roots. Have you ever eaten a carrot, radish, or beet? If so, you have eaten a root with stored food.

Different kinds of plants have different kinds of roots. Some plants have one large main root and other smaller roots. The large main root is called a **taproot.** Other plants have many roots that are all about the same size. These roots are **fibrous** (fī′brəs) **roots.** Look at the drawing. Which plants have fibrous roots? Which plants have a taproot?

dandelion   wheat   beet   cattail

Another kind of root is the prop root. **Prop roots** are extra roots that grow out from the sides of stems. On some trees they grow downward from the tree branches. Corn plants and mangrove (mang′grōv) trees have prop roots. How do you think prop roots got that name?

prop roots

Mangrove trees

Finding Out

Does more of a plant grow in the ground, or above the ground?

Get a potted plant. Take the plant out of the pot. Wash the soil off the roots with water. Then lay the plant on newspaper and carefully spread the roots and leaves.

Draw a circle around the roots. Draw another circle around the part of the plant that was above the ground. Cut along the lines you drew.

Compare the sizes of the two circles. Which circle is larger? Does more of this plant grow in the ground, or above the ground?

Stems

What do stems do?

The stems of most plants grow above the ground. They support, or hold up, the leaves, flowers, and other plant parts. Usually stems grow upward. But strawberries and some other plants have stems that grow along the ground. In still other plants, part of the stem grows underground. A potato is a stem that grows underground.

Strawberries

Zinnias

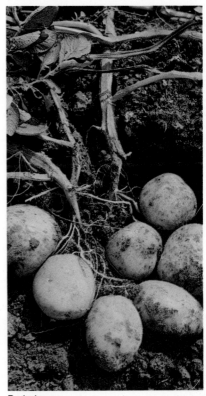
Potatoes

As you know, plants need water and minerals. These materials are taken in by the roots and are carried to the stem. Stems have tiny tubes like those in roots. Water and minerals are carried in those tubes to all parts of the plant. Look at the pictures. How do they show that stems carry materials to another part of the plant? The red, white, and blue flower was all white, like the one at the left. But its stem was split into three parts. Each part carried water of a different color to the flower.

There are four main kinds of seed plants. They are (1) trees, (2) shrubs, (3) herbs (ėrbz), and (4) vines. Each has a different kind of stem.

Most **trees** have one main stem called a trunk. The trunk is a woody stem. It is stiff and hard and covered with bark. Maples, oaks, and pines are common types of trees.

A **shrub** is smaller than a tree and has many woody stems. Some shrubs are called bushes. Rosebushes and lilac (lī′lək) bushes are types of shrubs.

Pine tree

French lilac bush

Sugar maple tree

45

Field of grass

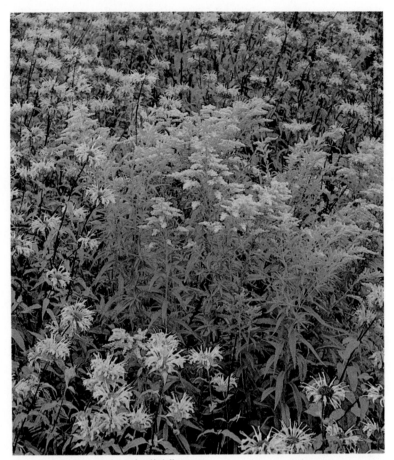
Goldenrod in field of wild flowers

Trout lily

An **herb** is another kind of seed plant. Herbs are small plants with soft rather than woody stems. Many herbs die at the end of one growing season. Grasses, flowers, and most weeds are types of herbs. Goldenrod is a weed that is an herb.

Many different herbs are used as food. Some people even have herb gardens. Have you ever eaten herbs such as parsley (pärs′lē) or chives (chīvz)?

Pumpkin

English ivy

A **vine** is another kind of plant with a soft stem. Vines cannot stand by themselves. They climb by wrapping around other things or they creep along the ground. Cucumber, pumpkin, and ivy are vines.

Do You Know?

Bamboo (bam bü') is a grass that can grow as tall as a tree. But it has a hollow stem. Some stems may be more than 20 centimeters across. Bamboo grows very quickly. One kind grows more than 2 centimeters in an hour. Bamboo is used in many ways. The seeds, leaves, and young plants are used as food. The stems are used to make such things as furniture, paper, and baskets.

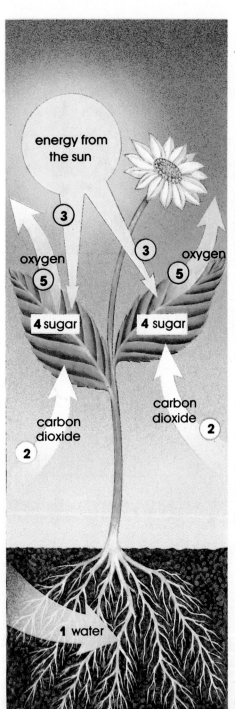

energy from
the sun

③

oxygen
⑤

4 sugar

carbon
dioxide

2

③

oxygen
⑤

4 sugar

carbon
dioxide

2

1 water

Leaves

What do leaves do?

Green plants make their own food. Most of the food is made in the leaves of plants. The leaves of plants can be compared to a factory. Materials must be brought to a factory before a product can be made. What materials might a factory need? How do materials get to a factory?

A leaf also needs certain materials before food can be made. Look at the drawing. (1) One thing the leaf needs is water. Water is taken in through the roots and carried to the leaf by stems. (2) A leaf also needs a gas from the air called **carbon dioxide** (kär′bən dī ok′sīd). Carbon dioxide enters the leaf through small openings on the leaf's surface. (3) Both green plants and factories need energy. Factories get energy by burning coal or other fuels. Plants get energy from the sun. (4) The food made by plants is sugar. Plants use the food they make to live and grow. How do you use food made by plants? A plant also gives off a gas called **oxygen** (ok′sə jən) when it makes food. Oxygen is needed by most living things to stay alive.

Banana plant

Juniper

American elm tree

Palm

Some leaves are large, and others are small. Large leaves can make more food than small leaves can make.

Leaves have different shapes. Look at these pictures of leaves. Some are shaped like spines. Some are long and flat with a smooth edge. Still others have a toothlike edge. Some leaves even have a shape like the scales of a fish. People use the shapes of leaves to tell one kind of plant from another. Why do leaves have different shapes?

Saguaro cactus

How are some leaves different from others?

LEAF SHAPES

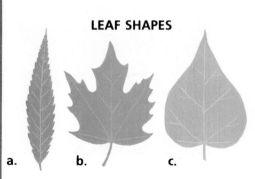

a.   b.   c.

LEAF EDGES

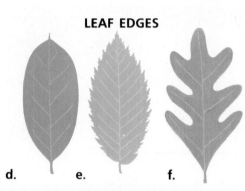

d.   e.   f.

VEIN PATTERNS

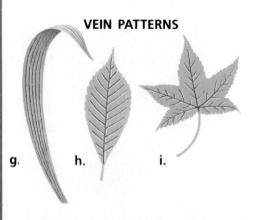

g.   h.   i.

Materials   leaf from 2 different kinds of plants

Procedure

A. Look at the shape of each leaf you have. Some leaves are narrow and some are wide. Some leaves are short and some are long. Some leaves are rounded and some have points. Compare your leaves with the drawings that show leaf shapes.

   1. What is the shape of each of your leaves?

B. Look at the edge of each leaf. Different kinds of leaves have different edges. The edges may be smooth, toothed, or lobed. Compare your leaves with the leaves in the drawings.

   2. What kind of edge does each of your leaves have?

C. Different leaves have different patterns of veins. Some leaves have veins that all start at the stem. Some leaves have one large vein and many smaller veins. Some leaves have many branching veins. Compare your leaves with the drawings that show vein patterns.

   3. Which of these vein patterns does each of your leaves have?

D. Draw a picture of each of your leaves. Show the shape of the leaf, the kind of edge, and the vein pattern.

Conclusion

In what ways are your two leaves different from each other?

Flowers and Seeds

What do flowers and seeds do?

Many green plants are seed plants. Some, such as trees and shrubs, live for many years. Others, such as most herbs, live only one growing season and then die.

Seeds may be formed in different ways. Most seed plants first produce flowers. The flowers form on the stems.

Forsythia

Summer at the pond

Alyssum

Autumn at the pond

Flowering crab tree

51

How apples form

Pea pods

As a flower grows, it slowly changes. After a while the outside parts of the flower dry up and fall off. At the same time, the inside part begins to grow. It changes into a fruit. The seeds form inside the fruit.

When you think of a fruit, you probably think of an apple or a pear. But walnuts, melons, and pea pods are fruits also. Even a milkweed pod is a fruit. What other fruits can you name? You probably have eaten many different fruits. Some fruits are good to eat, but many are not. A fruit such as a milkweed pod should not be eaten.

Have you ever seen plants like those in the pictures below? They are seed plants, but they do not produce flowers. They produce cones instead. The seeds form inside the cones. When the cones dry, they open and the seeds fall out.

Seeds in a honeydew melon

Cones on a tree

Dry cone with seeds

53

Seeds have many different shapes and sizes. But all seeds are alike in one way—they can produce new plants. How are the seeds in the pictures different?

Each seed has a covering called the **seed coat.** Inside the seed coat is a small plant. The plant has a tiny root, stem, and leaf. There is also stored food in the seed. Find these parts of the seed in the drawing.

Beggar-ticks

Shagbark hickory nuts

Milkweed pods and seeds

Cottonwood pods and seeds

A seed can produce a new plant only if it germinates (jėr′mə nāts). The seed **germinates** when the tiny plant inside begins to grow. This happens only when conditions are right. What do you think those conditions are? As the tiny plant grows, it uses the stored food in the seed. Later, when the plant has grown leaves, it will make its own food.

small plant

seed coat

stored food

OPENED BEAN SEED

GERMINATION AND GROWTH

Do seeds germinate at the same time?

Materials   paper towels / water / small jar / 3 radish seeds / 3 grass seeds / 3 corn seeds

Procedure

A. Fold a paper towel into a strip. The strip should be as wide as the jar is high.

B. Wet the paper towel and place it around the inside of the jar. Then fill the jar with crushed wet paper towels.

C. Carefully put three radish seeds between the jar and the strip of paper towel. In a different place, put three grass seeds between the jar and the towel. In another place, put three corn seeds.
  1. Which kind of seeds do you think will germinate first?
  2. Which kind of seeds do you think will germinate last?

D. Make a chart like the one shown.

E. Look at the jar each day. Keep the paper towels wet. Watch for the seeds to change. Write the changes that you see in your chart.
  3. Why should you keep the paper towels in the jar wet?

Conclusion

1. Did the radish seeds all germinate at the same time? Did the grass seeds? Did the corn seeds?
2. Did the three kinds of seeds germinate at the same time?

Date	Radish seeds	Grass seeds	Corn seeds

Ideas to Remember

▶ Seed plants are green plants.

▶ Most seed plants have the same plant parts—roots, stems, leaves, flowers, and seeds.

▶ Roots hold a plant in place. They also take in water for the plant.

▶ Stems support the plant parts that grow above the ground. Water and other materials are carried in the stems to other parts of the plant.

▶ Seed plants make their own food. The food is usually made in the leaves.

▶ Seed plants produce seeds from which new plants grow.

Reviewing the Chapter

A. Use all the terms below to fill in the blanks.

carbon dioxide	vines	herbs
shrubs	tree	oxygen

There are four main kinds of seed plants. A __1__ has one main woody stem called a trunk. Rosebushes have may woody stems and are called __2__. Plants with soft stems that cannot stand by themselves are called __3__. Plants such as grasses have soft stems also. These plants are called __4__.

All of these plants make their own food in their green leaves. The food is made from water and a gas called __5__. As the leaves make food, they give off a gas called __6__. Most living things need this gas to stay alive.

B. Write the meaning of these terms. Use each term in a sentence.

1. seed coat   **2.** taproot   **3.** germinates   **4.** fibrous roots   **5.** prop roots

UNDERSTANDING IDEAS

A. Make a chart like the one shown. Write the name of each plant in the correct place in the chart.

pumpkin	lilac bush	maple	cucumber	ivy
pine	goldenrod	grass	rosebush	oak

Trees	Shrubs	Herbs	Vines

B. Use the terms below to label the drawing. Describe what each part does for the plant.

root   stem   leaf
flower   seed

USING IDEAS

Get a leaf from a plant that grows outdoors. Tape it to a sheet of paper. Next to the leaf, make a drawing of the plant. Find out what the name of the plant is. Read about the plant's roots, leaves, and other parts. Then write a story that the plant might tell to describe itself.

THINKING LIKE A SCIENTIST

You may be able to answer some of these questions just by thinking about them. To answer other questions, you may have to do some research.

1. Plants that grow very close together are often much smaller than those that grow farther apart. Give some reasons why this happens.
2. Gardners often move plants from one place to another. When they do this, they are careful to take all of the plant's roots. Why is it important to do this? Plants can always grow new roots.
3. When a plant stem is cut, a heavy covering forms over the cut. This covering keeps water from leaking out of the plant. Why, then, do florists tell people to cut flower stems again before putting them into a vase of water?

Chapter 4

Plants Are Important

Think of what the world would be like if there were no plants. Would you have food? Would you have clothing? Would you have a place to live?

Look at the picture. Do you see any plants? Look again. There are many things in the picture that come from plants or parts of plants. Name those that you find.

Of all living things, plants are the most important. In this chapter you will learn why plants are so important. Also, you will find out some ways that plants or parts of plants are used.

Food from Plants

How are plants used as food?

As you know, green plants make their own food. You learned that carbon dioxide and water are changed into sugar in the leaves. Usually more sugar is made than the plant can use. The extra sugar is changed into starch (stärch) and other plant products. **Starch** is the stored food in seeds. It may also be stored in roots, stems, and leaves.

Potatoes

Carrots

Peanuts

Beets

Lettuce

Green plants are used as food by many living things. Many of the foods you eat are parts of green plants. Cabbage, lettuce, and spinach are plant leaves. Potatoes and asparagus (ə spar′ə gəs) are stems. Radishes, beets, and carrots are roots. Peaches, tomatoes, and cucumbers are fruits. Corn, dry beans, and peanuts are seeds. How many of these foods have you eaten? What other leaves, stems, roots, fruits, and seeds are foods?

Corn

Spinach

Tomatoes

Cucumbers

Asparagus

Cabbage

Radishes

How can you show there is starch in a green leaf?

Materials cornstarch / potted plant /alcohol / iodine solution / small beaker / petri dish / pencil / 2 paper towels

Procedure

A. Iodine is used to test for starch. Place some cornstarch on a paper towel. Put a drop of iodine solution on the cornstarch. *Caution: Iodine stains and is harmful if swallowed.*
  1. What color is the cornstarch?
  2. What color is the cornstarch after you put iodine solution on it?

B. Pick a leaf off a plant. Lay it on a paper towel on your desk. Roll a pencil over the leaf several times. Press hard as you do this.

C. Place the leaf in a beaker. Pour alcohol into the beaker until the leaf is covered. *Caution: This kind of alcohol is harmful if swallowed.* Let the leaf soak overnight.

D. Take the leaf out of the alcohol and place it in a petri dish.
  3. What color is the alcohol?
  4. What color is the leaf?
  5. What do you think will happen if you cover the leaf with iodine solution?

E. Cover the leaf with iodine solution.
  6. Describe what happens to the leaf.

Conclusion

Is there starch in the green leaf? Where did the starch come from?

Sometimes you may not recognize a food as being part of a plant. Breakfast foods such as oatmeal and cornflakes are made from seeds. Flour is also made from seeds. These foods are made from seeds called grains (grānz). **Grains** are the seeds of certain grasses such as oats and corn. Wheat and rice are other examples of grains. Many different kinds of grains are used as food by both people and animals.

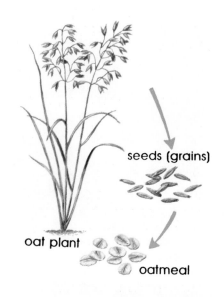

seeds (grains)

oat plant

oatmeal

Wheat field

Rice field

Coffee seeds (beans)

Tea leaves

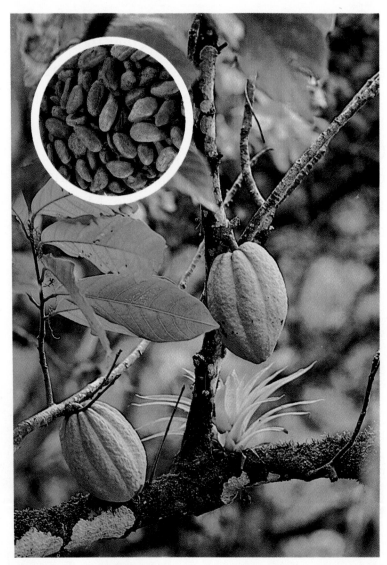

Cacao seeds and pods

Do you drink cocoa or hot chocolate? Cocoa and chocolate are made from the seeds of the cacao (kə kā′ō) tree. Coffee is also made from the seeds of a certain kind of tree. The leaves of still other kinds of trees are used to make tea.

Seeds, as well as the fruits of some plants, contain oil. Some of those oils are used for cooking. Corn oil is such an oil. What other cooking oils can you name?

Do you use mustard? Mustard is a spice used to flavor foods. Cloves, nutmeg, pepper, and cinnamon (sin'ə mən) are also spices. These and other spices come from plants.

Often a single kind of plant is used as food in different ways. Look at the drawing of the corn plant. What are some of the ways it is used as food?

Mushroom

Most people eat some foods that are not parts of green plants. Do you eat meat and eggs? Do you drink milk? These foods come from animals that eat green plants. Without green plants, there would be no meat, milk, or eggs.

Some plants used for food are not green plants. Look at the pictures. Have you ever eaten plants like these? These plants are mushrooms. Most of the mushrooms that people eat are grown on mushroom farms.

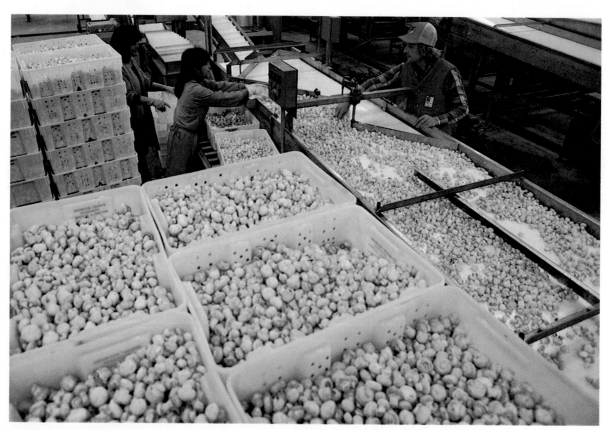

Mushroom farm

How can you tell
if a fruit or a seed contains oil?

Materials brown paper bag / scissors / crayon / 2 toothpicks / water / cooking oil / walnut or peanut / olive / sunflower seed / orange peel or lemon peel / apple

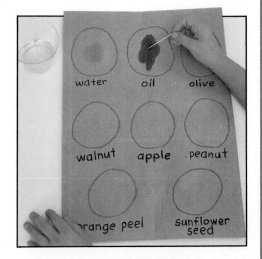

Procedure

A. Cut out a large piece from a brown paper bag. Using a crayon, draw circles on the brown paper. You will need at least seven circles.

B. Use a toothpick to put a drop of water in one circle. Use another toothpick to put a drop of cooking oil in another circle. Label these circles *water* and *oil.*

C. In each of the other circles, place a piece of a fruit or a piece of a crushed seed. Write the name of the fruit or seed below the circle.

   1. Which of these fruits and seeds do you think contain oil?

D. Press down hard with your thumb on each piece of fruit or seed. Press on one piece at a time. Be sure to wash and dry your fingers before each test.

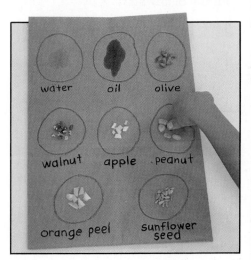

E. Take the fruits and seeds off the paper. Wait for the paper to dry. Then hold it up to a light.

Results

Which fruits and seeds contain oil?

Conclusion

How were you able to tell if a fruit or a seed contains oil?

Other Uses of Plants

How are plants used other than as food?

Bouquet of flowers

You may think that plants are important only as food. But they are also important in other ways.

Plants are often used for decoration. Many people grow house plants because they are pretty or they smell nice. Flowers help to make a room look bright and cheerful.

Plants are also used for decoration outdoors. What kinds of plants are used for decoration in this picture?

Plants for decoration outdoors

Sometimes plants that are grown for decoration are also used in other ways, such as for shade. In some places, rows of trees are used as windbreaks. Other trees and shrubs are used as living fences. Grass and other plants growing on a hillside help to hold the soil in place.

Grass clippings, leaves, and other plant parts can be made into compost (kom′pōst). **Compost** is rotted plant material. When compost is mixed into the soil, it returns minerals to the soil. It also helps to hold water in the soil.

Trees used as a windbreak

Compost pile

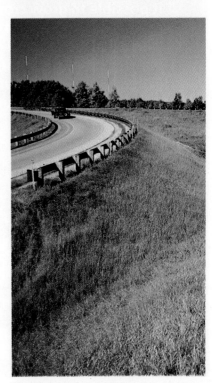

Plants used to hold soil

71

Penicillin mold

Many medicines come from plants. Have you ever had to take penicillin (pen ə sil'in)? Penicillin is a medicine made from a certain kind of mold. Oil of wintergreen and castor oil come from other kinds of plants. Many of the medicines used to ease pain are made from plants.

Some plants produce materials that are made into cloth for clothing. You may be wearing some clothing made of cotton. The

Science & Technology

▶ A new kind of farming may make it possible to grow crops without soil. This kind of farming is called hydroponics (hī drə pon′ iks). Plants usually get minerals from the soil. When plants are grown by hydroponics, the minerals can be put into the water.

◀ Small hydroponic crops, such as peppers and lettuce, are now being grown. This is done indoors where sunlight and temperature are controlled. Growing tables that hold water are used. In what parts of the world will hydroponics be most useful?

Cotton plant

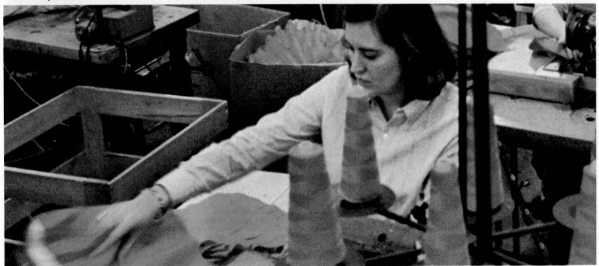
Clothing factory

cotton fibers (fī'bərz) that are woven into cloth are produced by the seeds of the cotton plant. Rope and bags are also made from plant fibers. Other plant materials are made into such things as rayon (rā'on) cloth and brooms.

Rope, broom, and canvas bag

Paper products

Charcoal

Tapped rubber tree

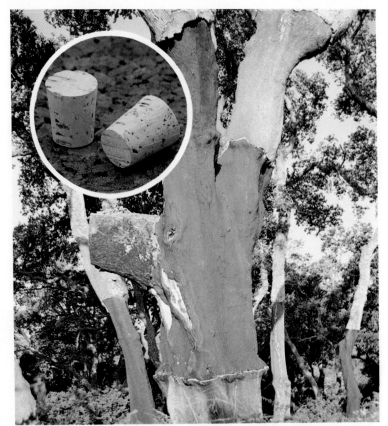
Cork products and stripped cork tree

Anything made of wood comes from trees. Many kinds of trees are used for lumber. Paper and charcoal are also made from wood. Rubber, chewing gum, and cork come from trees. Many trees produce oils that are made into waxes and paints. Many dyes (dīz) used to color cloth and to make ink are products of trees.

The ways that plants are used is almost endless. What other uses of plants can you think of?

Harmful Plants

How are some plants harmful?

Although many plants are useful, some other plants are harmful. Most molds spoil food. You probably have seen mold growing on fruit and other foods.

Another harmful plant is mildew (mil'dü). **Mildew** is a nongreen plant that grows in shady damp places. Often it is found growing on leather, painted surfaces, water pipes, and basement walls. You may have seen it growing in the bathroom around the tub or shower. Like some molds, mildew ruins the things it grows on.

Mold growing on oranges

Mildew growing on leather

Some green plants are harmful, too. These plants may be found growing in the woods and in fields. They also may be found in your home, in your yard, or in a park. Often these plants can cause illness or death if they are eaten. Sometimes only part of a plant is harmful. Sometimes the whole plant may be harmful. Just touching some plants can make your skin blister and itch.

SOME HARMFUL PLANTS YOU SHOULD KNOW

Plant	Harmful part	How it is harmful
Poison ivy	All	Touching
Poinsettia	Leaves, stem, and milky sap	Eating
Yew	All	Eating
Holly	Berries	Eating
Buttercup	All	Eating
Some mushrooms	All	Eating

What does bread mold look like?

Sprinkle a few drops of water on a small piece of bread. Then wipe the bread on a dusty floor. Lay the bread with the dusty side up in a clear plastic jar or in a clear plastic sandwich bag. Cover the jar tightly, and place it in a warm dark place. Mold should grow on the bread in a few days. Without opening the jar, look at the mold with a hand lens. What does the bread mold look like? What color is it? What does the mold use for food?

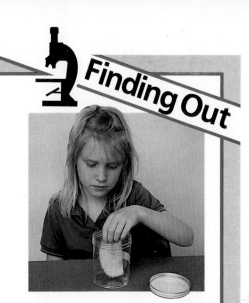

Ideas to Remember

- ▶ Green plants are used as food by many living things.
- ▶ The roots, stems, leaves, fruits, or seeds of some plants are used for food.
- ▶ A mushroom is a nongreen plant used for food.
- ▶ Plants are useful in many ways other than as food.
- ▶ Among the many things made from plants are lumber, waxes, clothing, and paper.
- ▶ Some plants are not safe to eat or touch.

Reviewing the Chapter

A. Unscramble each group of letters to find a science term from the chapter. Then copy the sentences below. Use one term to complete each sentence.

   1. nagisr   **2.** thacsr   **3.** ptocmso

   4. Rotted plant material is called ____.
   5. Seeds of certain grasses, such as oats and corn, are called ____.
   6. The stored food in seeds is called ____.

B. Write the letter of the term that best matches the definition. Not all the terms will be used.

1. Returns minerals to the soil	**a.** starch
2. Nongreen plants that are used for food	**b.** mustard
	c. milk
3. A spice	**d.** mildew
4. A harmful plant often found growing in basements and bathrooms	**e.** mushrooms
	f. compost
5. Seeds used for breakfast foods	**g.** grains
	h. cotton
6. A medicine from a plant	**i.** penicillin
7. A food from some animals	
8. Plant fibers that can be woven into cloth	

UNDERSTANDING IDEAS

A. Describe three uses of plants other than as food.

B. Describe three ways plants can be harmful.

C. All the foods named below are parts of green plants. Make a chart like the one shown. Write the name of each food in the correct place in the chart.

tomato   cucumber   radish   carrot   spinach
lettuce   rhubarb   cocoa   corn   potato
coffee   dry beans   cabbage   peach   beet

Leaf	Stem	Fruit	Seed	Root

USING IDEAS

Draw a picture like the one shown. Use crayons to draw plants in your picture. Show how you would use plants for decoration, for a windbreak, for holding soil in place, and for shade. Draw a vegetable garden, too.

THINKING LIKE A SCIENTIST

You may be able to answer some of these questions just by thinking about them. To answer other questions, you may have to do some research.

1. Fruits such as peaches and apples form on trees in late spring and early summer. Why, then, is frost in early spring harmful to these plants?

2. Many years ago, toys were not bought in stores. They were made at home. Name some toys you could make from parts of plants.

Science in Careers

An interest in plants and animals can lead to many kinds of jobs. **Gardeners** plant trees, shrubs, and flowers. They must know which plants will grow best in different places.

Park rangers and **game wardens** protect wild animals from people who could harm them.

Foresters

Park ranger

Foresters care for the trees in forests. They choose the trees that will be cut down and made into lumber and paper. They also fight forest fires and plant new trees.

Botanists (bot'ə nists) are scientists who study plants and plant life. They try to learn new things about plants. Some botanists try to find out how to make plants grow faster or bigger. Then try to find how to get more food from plants.

Botanist

People in Science

JANE VAN LAWICK-GOODALL
(1934–   )

Jane van Lawick-Goodall is a zoologist (zō ol′ə jist). She studies the behavior of animals such as baboons and chimpanzees. She studies the animals at close range as they live in the wild. She observes what the animals do and how they get along with each other.

Baboons living in the wild

Developing Skills

WORD SKILLS

The important science terms used in this book are listed in the Glossary. The Glossary is found at the back of the book. It gives the meanings of the terms.

Use the Glossary to answer these questions.

1. In what order are the terms in the Glossary listed?

2. What other information is in the Glossary?

3. Use the Glossary to find the meaning of the term *grain.*

4. Use the Glossary to find the meaning of the term *sleet.*

There is also an Index at the back of this book. The Index is a list of important topics.

Subtopics are listed below the main topic.

Use the Index to answer these questions.

1. In what order are the topics listed?

2. On what pages can you find information about stems?

3. On what pages can you find information about inclined planes?

4. What subtopics are listed for the topic of roots?

READING A BAR GRAPH

A bar graph can be used to compare things. Look at the bar graph on the next page. It compares the number of blue whales found in the world from 1900 to 1980. Use the bar graph to answer the following questions.

1. How many whales were there in 1900?

2. How many whales were there in 1940?

3. How many whales were there in 1980?

4. In which year were more whales found, 1910 or 1950?

5. In which year were fewer whales found, 1920 or 1930?

6. What is the difference between the number of whales found in 1940 and the number of whales found in 1970?

82

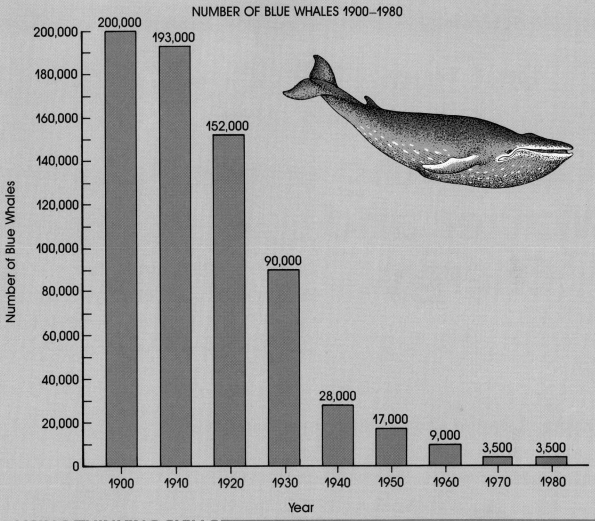

NUMBER OF BLUE WHALES 1900–1980

Number of Blue Whales (y-axis), Year (x-axis)

- 1900: 200,000
- 1910: 193,000
- 1920: 152,000
- 1930: 90,000
- 1940: 28,000
- 1950: 17,000
- 1960: 9,000
- 1970: 3,500
- 1980: 3,500

USING THINKING SKILLS

Whales are important to many people. Some people believe that whales should be hunted. People can get oil, meat, and blubber from whales. Other people feel that whales should be protected from hunters. Think about this as you answer these questions.

1. Why do you think there are so many fewer whales in the world now than in 1900?

2. Would anything happen if there were no more whales?

3. Should whales be hunted? Should whales be protected? Explain your answer.

Unit Two

Observing Matter and Energy

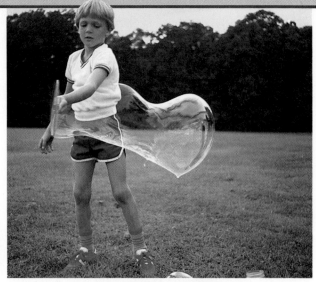

Chapter 5—All About Matter
Everything is made of matter. Matter can be a solid, a liquid, or a gas. What kind of matter is inside a bubble?

Chapter 8—Sound   A megaphone (meg'ə fōn) is used to make a voice sound louder. The cone shape of the megaphone directs the sound and keeps it from spreading out. This chapter will tell you all about sound.

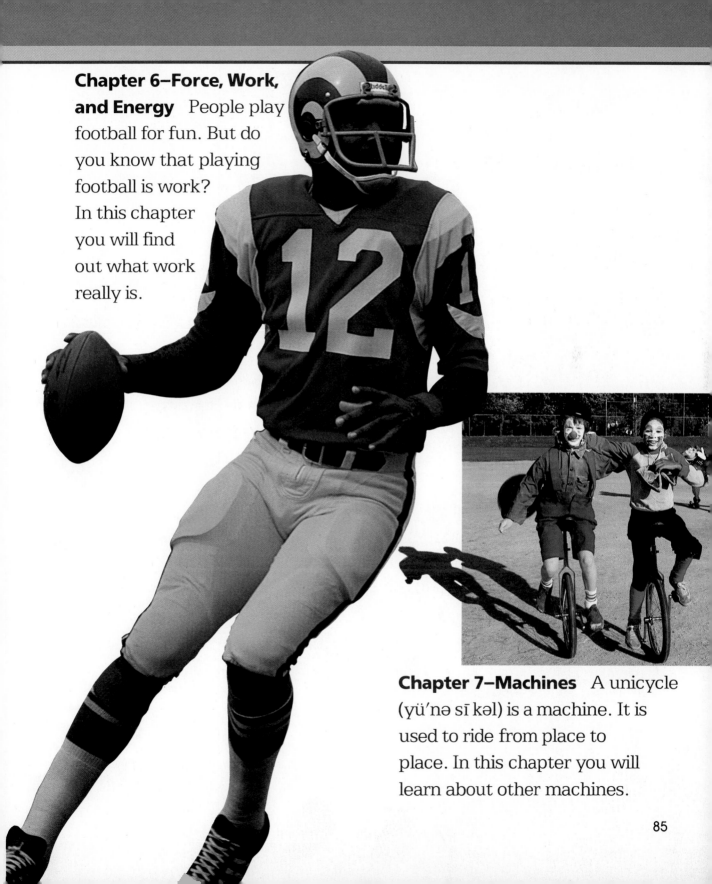

Chapter 6–Force, Work, and Energy   People play football for fun. But do you know that playing football is work? In this chapter you will find out what work really is.

Chapter 7–Machines   A unicycle (yü′nə sī kəl) is a machine. It is used to ride from place to place. In this chapter you will learn about other machines.

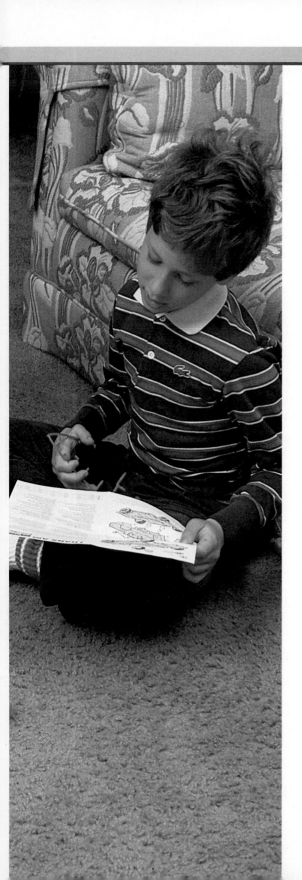

Chapter 5

All About Matter

Putting a model together can be fun. These children are looking for pieces that will fit together. After all the pieces have been put in the right places, they will form a model car.

Do you know that everything around you is made of small pieces? But the pieces are so small that you cannot see them. Like the pieces of the model, they are joined in a special way.

In this chapter you will learn about the small pieces that form all of the things around you.

Properties of Matter

What is matter?

Look at the objects on the table. You probably use objects like these every day. They look very different from each other. But they are all alike in one way. They are all made of **matter.**

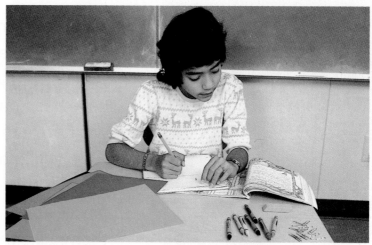

Many kinds of matter

Each object on the table has a different color and size. And each has a different shape. Color, size, and shape are properties (prop'ər tēz). Different properties help you tell these things apart.

The objects on the table have other properties, too. All of them take up space. Which object takes up the most space? Which one takes up the least space?

The objects on the table are different in another way. Some are heavier than others. They have more mass. **Mass** is a measure of how much matter there is in an object.

All matter takes up space and has mass. If you look around, you will see many kinds of matter. You yourself take up space and have mass. So you are made of matter, too.

Sometimes you can see how much space matter takes up. But you cannot see how much mass it has. These children are finding the mass of a book. To do this, they are using a balance (bal'əns). A **balance** is a tool that is used to measure mass.

Measuring mass

Activity

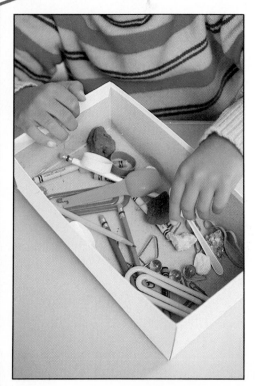

What are some properties of matter?

Materials a box of assorted objects

Procedure

A. Look at the objects in the box. They are all made of matter.

B. Color is one property of matter. Use this property to put the objects into groups.
   1. What are the colors of the groups?

C. Think of another property of matter. Use this property to put the objects into new groups.
   2. How are the objects in each group alike?

D. Repeat step **C.** See how many different ways you can group the objects.

E. Compare your groups with those of other students.

Conclusion

1. What are some properties of matter?
2. How many properties did you identify?

Using science ideas

Make a collection of objects such as rocks, leaves, or stamps. Use their properties to group the objects.

States of Matter

What are the states of matter?

Have you ever blown up a balloon? If you have, you know that you filled the balloon with air. The air takes up space and it has mass. The air inside the balloon is made of matter.

Matter can be found in different forms. Matter may be a solid or a liquid (lik'wid). Or, like the air inside the balloon, matter may be a gas. The states of matter are **solid, liquid,** and **gas.**

You can see all three states of matter in this fish tank. The glass tank is solid matter. The water inside the tank is liquid matter. And the air bubbles are filled with gas.

Filling a balloon

A solid, a liquid, and a gas

Now look around. Name things you see that are solid, liquid, or gas. You may see many solids and liquids. But most times you cannot see gas.

Each state of matter has different properties. Solids have a shape of their own. The shape of most solids does not change. But solids are found in many different shapes. Look at the rocks this boy has collected. Rocks are solid. Look at the different shapes of the rocks.

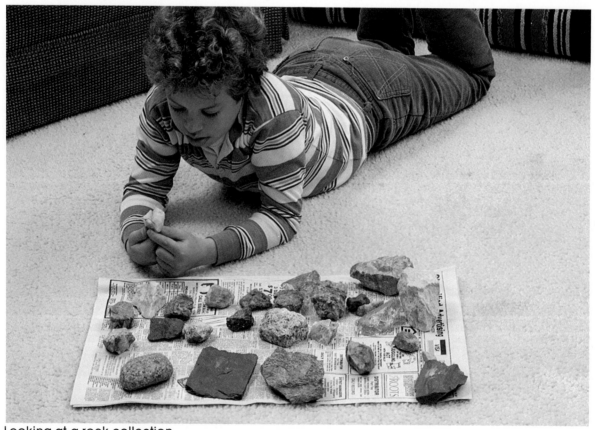

Looking at a rock collection

Liquids are not like solids. Liquids never have a shape of their own. They always have the same shape as their container. This means that the same liquid in different containers will have different shapes. In the picture you can see milk in the glass and in the straw. The milk changes shape as it is moved from the glass up through the straw. When all the milk is gone, what do you think will fill the glass and the straw? Both will be filled with another kind of matter, a gas.

Liquid changing shape

Like liquids, gases also have the same shape as their container. Each of these objects has a different shape. The gas in each object has the same shape as the object it fills.

Gas-filled objects

The Particles in Matter

What is matter made of?

Why are solids, liquids, and gases so different from each other? To answer this, you must learn more about matter. All matter is made of small particles (pär'tə kəlz) called **atoms** (at'əmz). There are many kinds of atoms. They are so small that you cannot see them. Atoms join together in different ways to form larger particles of matter. Many of these particles join to form the matter around you.

In the drawings you can see how close particles are in different states of matter. In the solid they are close together. In the liquid they are farther apart. And in the gas they are even farther apart.

The particles in matter are always moving. But you cannot see them or feel them move. Look at the drawings. The arrows show how much the particles in matter move. In solids, the close particles move back and forth, or vibrate. But they never change places. This is why most solids do not change shape. The particles in liquids move more than those in solids. They slide over each other. This is why liquids have no shape of their own. The particles in gases move the most. They bump into each other. They spread out to fill any container. The states of matter are different because the particles in them behave differently.

Finding Out

How can you show that the particles in a liquid are moving?

Pour some warm water into a jar. Use warm water from a faucet. Do not fill the jar to the top. Put the jar in a place where it will not be moved. Now place a tea bag into the water so that it hangs just below the surface of the water. To hold the tea bag in place, tape the string on the tea bag to the outside of the jar. Watch what happens to the water. Look at the water again in a few minutes. Let the jar of water stand overnight. Look at the water the next day. Describe how the appearance of the water has changed. Explain why the water changed.

Matter Can Change

How does matter change?

Matter can change from one state to another. This kind of change is called a **physical** (fiz′ə kəl) **change.** Changes in size and shape are also physical changes. In a physical change, you have the same kind of matter before and after the change.

Water is matter. When water is poured, it is a liquid. If the water is put into a freezer, it changes to ice. If the water is heated enough, it will form a gas. Water in the form of a gas is called **water vapor** (vā′pər).

Changing size and shape

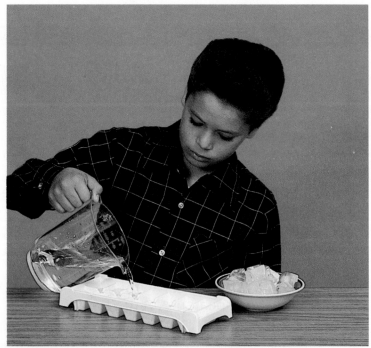
Liquid water and ice

These changes in water show that matter can change from a liquid to a solid. It also shows that a liquid can change to a gas. Water may change from one state to another. But it is always water. It never changes to anything else.

Ice starts to form when water is cooled to zero degrees Celsius (sel'sē əs). (The symbol for degrees Celsius is °C.) This temperature (tem'pər ə chər) is the **freezing point** of water. At 0°C, the moving particles in water slow down to form ice. The water in this pond is frozen. How will the ice change on a warm day?

Frozen pond

Icicle melting

Water begins to boil at 100°C. This is the **boiling point** of water. As water boils, its particles move faster and farther apart. The particles then escape to form steam.

Water evaporating

Water condensing

In the picture, steam is rising from boiling water. But water does not have to boil to change to a gas. Moving particles of water are always escaping from the surface to form water vapor. This change in the water from a liquid to a gas is called **evaporation** (i vap ə rā'shen).

Water vapor can change back to a liquid. This kind of change is called **condensation** (kon den sā'shən). Condensation takes place when water vapor is cooled. If you breathe on a cool window, water vapor from your breath changes into liquid water.

Science & TECHNOLOGY

▶ In many parts of the world there is not enough fresh water for people to drink. But there is a lot of fresh water in icebergs.

Scientists have thought of a way to move an iceberg to where it is needed. First, the iceberg could be covered with plastic insulation (in sə lā'shən) so it would not melt. Then tugboats and helicopters could tow the iceberg.

So far, this idea has not been tried. Do you have a better idea? What is it?

Different Kinds of Matter

How can one kind of matter become different matter?

You learned that matter, such as water, may change from one state to another. This is a physical change. Matter may change in another way.

Firewood

Burning wood

Ashes

Some matter can become different matter. This kind of change is called a **chemical** (kem′ə kəl) **change.** Burning causes wood to change to ashes. In the pictures you can see that wood and ashes do not look the same. Is there any way to change the ashes back to wood?

Activity

How can you cause a chemical change to take place?

Materials   bottle / 2 antacid tablets / balloon / water / funnel / measuring cup

Procedure

A. Break 2 antacid tablets into small pieces. Drop the pieces of tablet into a bottle.

B. Use a funnel to pour some water into a balloon.

C. Place the open end of the balloon over the opening in the bottle.
   1. What do you think will happen when the water falls into the bottle?

D. Lift the other end of the balloon so that water falls into the bottle.
   2. What do you see happening inside the bottle?
   3. What is happening to the balloon?

Results

1. What kind of matter formed inside the balloon?

2. Describe how the matter that formed inside the balloon is different from the water and the tablets.

Conclusion

1. What did you do to cause a chemical change to take place?

2. Do you think you would be able to change the matter that formed in the bottle and in the balloon back into water and tablets? Explain your answer.

Sometimes different matter is formed when two or more kinds of matter are mixed together. These children are making bread. To do this, they are mixing many special things together. The bread will not be like the things it is made from. The bread will be different matter.

Ideas to Remember

▶ Matter is anything that takes up space and has mass.
▶ The states of matter are solid, liquid, and gas.
▶ All matter is made of atoms.
▶ Some kinds of matter can change from one state to another.
▶ Some kinds of matter can become different matter.

Reviewing the Chapter

SCIENCE WORDS

A. Copy the sentences below. Use science terms from the chapter to complete the sentences.

1. The three states of matter are ____, ____, and ____.
2. The temperature 0°C is the ____ point of water.
3. New matter is formed in a ____ change.
4. Water in the form of a gas is called water ____.
5. The measure of how much matter there is in an object is called ____.
6. The temperature 100°C is the ____ point of water.
7. Melting is an example of a ____ change.

B. Write the letter of the term that best matches the definition. Not all the terms will be used.

1. Smallest particle of matter
2. The change from a gas to a liquid
3. Tool to measure mass
4. Matter that takes the shape of its container
5. The change from a liquid to a gas
6. Matter that has a shape of its own

   a. evaporation
   b. solid
   c. mass
   d. condensation
   e. atom
   f. liquid
   g. balance

UNDERSTANDING IDEAS

A. When you are at home, find out how different kinds of food are changed before they are eaten. Make a list of the changes you find. Next to each change write *P* if it describes a physical change. Write *C* it if describes a chemical change.

B. Write a recipe that uses two or more kinds of matter to make different matter. What is needed to make the matter change?

C. Make a chart like the one shown. Then look around your classroom. Find as many objects as you can that fit these groups. Write the names of these objects under the correct headings.

Solids	Liquids	Gases

USING IDEAS

Find out if all liquids have the same freezing point. Label two paper cups *A* and *B*. Half fill both cups with water. Put a teaspoon of salt into cup *A* and stir.

Put both cups into the freezer. Check the cups every half hour. Which cup of water starts to freeze first?

THINKING LIKE A SCIENTIST

You may be able to answer some of these questions just by thinking about them. To answer other questions, you may have to do some research.

1. When water gets very cold, it freezes into ice. Ice is a solid that is lighter than water. Why is it important to some fish that ice floats on water?

2. Draw two squares. Label one square *Water*. Label the other square *Ice*. In each square box, draw particles that show that state of matter. Tell how the particles in each square are different.

3. The following are chemical changes. What is needed to make each change take place?
   a. Wood to ashes
   b. Flour, water, and yeast to bread
   c. Baking soda to carbon dioxide
   d. Iron to rust

4. Predict what might happen if liquid were not a state of matter on the earth.

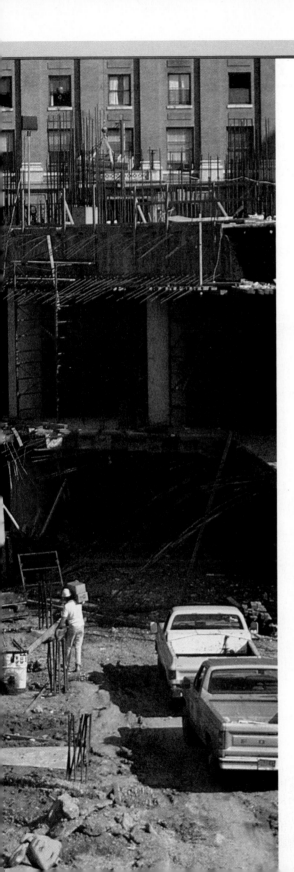

Chapter 6

Force, Work, and Energy

These people are putting up a new building. To do this job, they must move ground, cement, and steel. You can see that a lot of pushing, pulling, and lifting is needed. Some is being done by people and some is being done by machines. What things are being pushed or pulled? What things are being lifted?

In this chapter you will learn more about pushing, pulling, and lifting. You will also learn about the energy needed to do these things.

Forces

Look at the pictures. Sometimes you push to make things move, and sometimes you pull. You push or pull even when you lift something. A push or a pull is a **force** (fôrs). Force is always needed to make something move.

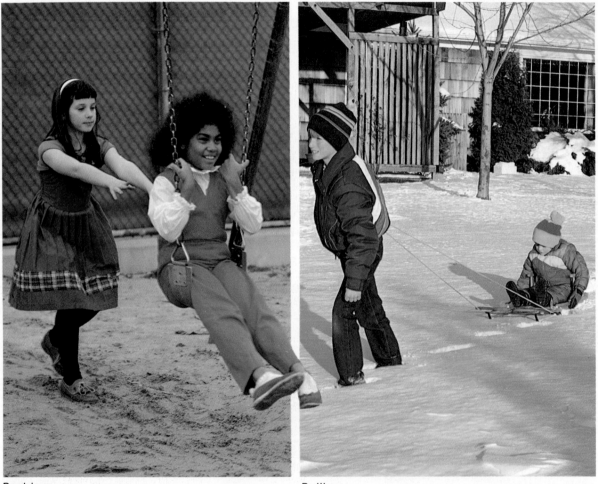

Pushing   Pulling

It takes more force to move some things than it does to move others. For example, suppose that you lifted a big dictionary. Then you lifted a smaller book. You would use a different amount of force to lift each one. Which would take more force to lift, the dictionary or the smaller book?

This boy is using a pulling force. He is using force not to make the dog move but to make it stop. Force must be used to make things slow down or stop moving.

In this picture the skier is using a pushing force on her pole to turn. Force must also be used to make moving things change their direction.

In all of these examples, forces change the motion of things. When something that is standing still starts to move, its motion changes. Stopping is a change in motion. Speeding up, slowing down, and turning are all changes in motion. Pushing or pulling forces are needed to cause all of these changes.

Kinds of Forces

What are some pushing and pulling forces?

Why is this diver falling toward the water? You cannot see anything pushing or pulling her. What is making her move? The force that is making the diver move is gravity (grav′ə tē). **Gravity** is the force of one object pulling on another object. The earth pulls on all things with this force. Rain, snow, and leaves always fall to the ground. A ball thrown into the air always falls to the ground. The earth's gravity pulls all these things toward the ground.

▶ Out in space, there is no gravity. People and objects float because they have no weight. Astronauts who go outside a spacecraft wear a jetpack. This is a jet-powered backpack. With it, an astronaut can move in space.

◀ Inside a spacecraft, astronauts do experiments. In some experiments, the astronauts do tests on their bodies. They hope to learn how weightlessness affects the body. Look in a library to find out about experiments done in space.

Measuring the pull of gravity

The earth's gravity pulls on some things more than on others. Objects with more mass are pulled more by the earth's gravity. For example, a bowling ball is pulled toward the earth more than a basketball is. The bowling ball has more mass.

When you weigh something, you are measuring the pull of the earth's gravity. Suppose you weigh 31 kilograms and a friend weighs 27 kilograms. Who is pulled more by gravity?

How can you measure the pull of gravity?

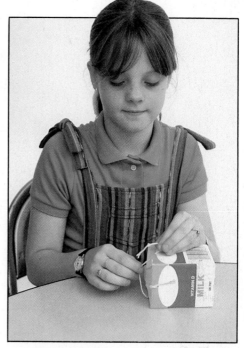

Materials small milk carton / scissors / 2 pieces of string, each 20 cm long / 2 wooden metric rulers / 3 books / rubber band / paper clip / 10 washers

Procedure

A. Cut off the top part of a milk carton. Make a hole in each side of the carton. Tie the ends of each piece of string through opposite holes in the milk carton.

B. Place a wooden ruler on a table so that one end of the ruler extends 10 cm over the edge of the table. Use the books to hold down the other end of the ruler.

C. Hook one end of a paper clip through the strings on the milk carton. Hook the other end of the paper clip to a rubber band. Then hang the rubber band over the free end of the ruler.

D. Measure the length of the rubber band.
   1. How long is the rubber band?

E. Put 2 washers into the carton.
   2. How long is the rubber band now?

F. Repeat step **E.** four more times. Each time, put 2 more washers into the carton.
   3. How long is the rubber band when there are 4, 6, 8, and 10 washers in the carton?

Results

What happened to the rubber band each time more washers were put into the carton?

Conclusion

How did the changes in the rubber band show the pull of gravity?

This picture shows another kind of force at work. The motion of the paper clips changed when they were lifted. Magnetism (mag'nə tiz əm) caused this change. **Magnetism** is a force that acts on some kinds of metal.

Magnet lifting paper clips

Different shapes and kinds of magnets

If you have ever used magnets, you know that magnetism is not like gravity. Gravity is only a pulling force. But magnetism sometimes pulls and sometimes pushes.

Magnets have two ends. They are called the north pole and the south pole. There is a pulling force between a north pole and a south pole. Two north poles or two south poles push each other away.

Have you ever played shuffleboard? After you push the disk, it slides across the floor. As it moves, it slows down until it stops. Slowing down and stopping are changes in the motion of the disk.

The force that causes this change in motion is friction (frik'shən). **Friction** is a force that slows down or stops motion. It is produced by one thing rubbing against another. If there were no friction, the shuffleboard disk would keep on moving.

PULLING AND PUSHING FORCES
BETWEEN THE POLES OF MAGNETS

Oiling a hinge

What happens when you rub your hands together? Do your hands feel warmer? Friction produces heat. Objects that rub always become warmer. What would happen if you made your hands slippery with soap and water? There would be less friction then. Your hands would not feel as warm. Something that reduces friction is called a **lubricant** (lü′brə kənt). Oil is one kind of lubricant. Grease is another kind of lubricant. What other lubricants can you name?

Finding Out

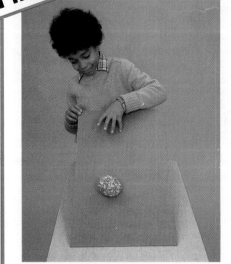

How is friction increased or reduced?

Make a slide from a piece of heavy smooth cardboard. Use books to prop up one end. Let a smooth flat stone go down the slide. Notice how fast it moves.

Lay the cardboard flat and rub one side with sandpaper to make it rough. Set up the slide again. Find out if the stone slides faster or slower on the rough cardboard.

Turn the cardboard over and lay it flat. Rub a bar of soap all over this side. Set up the slide again. Find out if the stone slides faster or slower than before.

When did the slide have the least friction? The most friction?

Work

Look at the picture. Where is work being done? **Work** is done when a force is used to move something. For example, you do work if you push a chair across a room. Suppose someone sat on the chair. Then you would have to push harder to move it. You would be using more force, so you would be doing more work.

115

FORCE × DISTANCE = WORK

force

2 meters

FORCE × GREATER DISTANCE = MORE WORK

force

4 meters

You also do more work if you move something a greater distance. Suppose that you move a chair 2 meters. The next time, you move it 4 meters. Four meters is a greater distance than 2 meters. When you move the chair 4 meters, you do more work.

The amount of work that is done always depends on two things. It depends on how much force is used to move an object. And it depends on how far the object moves. Look at the picture. Is the person pushing against the wall doing work? Why or why not?

Energy

How is energy used to do work?

Do you feel tired after you do work? You may feel that way because you have used up energy. **Energy** is the ability to do work. Energy is used whenever a force moves something.

There are many different kinds of energy. One kind is heat energy. In the picture heat energy is being used to make the balloon rise. So heat energy is being used to do work.

Electricity (i lek tris′ə tē) is another kind of energy. It is used to run a motor attached to the garage door. This motor puts a force on the door. The force moves the door upward. Work is done as the door moves.

Electric garage-door opener

Hot-air balloon

117

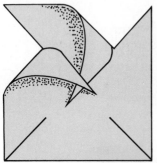

Activity

How can moving air be used to do work?

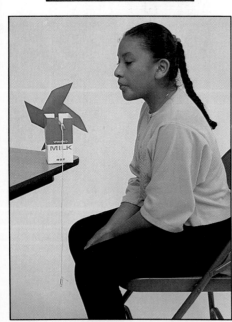

Materials construction paper, 15 cm × 15 cm / pushpin / pencil that has an eraser / string, 45 cm long / empty milk carton / scissors / paper clip / heavy object

Procedure

A. Cut the top off an empty milk carton. Then cut 2 deep U-shape grooves in opposite sides of the milk carton. Put a heavy object into the carton to weigh it down.

B. Tie a paper clip to one end of a piece of string. Tape the other end of the string to the writing end of a pencil.

C. Cut a piece of construction paper in 4 places, as shown. Then bend 4 points of the paper to the center.

D. Stick a pushpin through the center of the paper. Then stick the pin into the eraser on the pencil.

E. Set the pencil into the grooves of the milk carton. Place the milk carton at the edge of a table so that the paper clip on the string hangs freely.
   1. What do you think will happen when you blow on the blades of the windmill?

F. Now blow across the top of the windmill so that the blades catch the moving air.

Results
Describe what happens when you blow on the blades of the windmill.

Conclusion
How do you know that moving air can do work?

Some other kinds of energy are light, sound, and mechanical (mə kan′ə kəl) energy. Mechanical energy is the energy of moving bodies. An elevator has mechanical energy as it moves up and down. Water also has mechanical energy that can be used to do work. Look around you. Where do you see other examples of mechanical energy? You have mechanical energy also. You have it when you run, write with a pencil, or move in any way.

Outdoor elevators

Ideas to Remember

▶ A force is a push or a pull.
▶ Forces can change the motion of things.
▶ Gravity, magnetism, and friction are forces.
▶ Work is done when a force moves something.
▶ Energy is used to do work.
▶ Light, heat, electricity, sound, and mechanical energy are kinds of energy.

Waterwheel

Reviewing the Chapter

SCIENCE WORDS

A. Copy the sentences below. Use science terms from the chapter to complete the sentences.

1. The force that pulls things toward the earth is _____.
2. A material, such as oil, that reduces friction is called a _____.
3. A force that may be a push or a pull and that acts on certain metals is _____.
4. When a force is used to move something, _____ is done.
5. The force that slows down or stops the motion of objects that rub against one another is _____.

B. Identify each of the following.

1. I am used whenever a force moves something. I am the ability to do work. What am I?

2. I must be used to make moving things change their direction. I may be a push or a pull. What am I?

UNDERSTANDING IDEAS

A. Name three kinds of energy. Give an example of each.

B. The drawings show different things happening. For each drawing, name the force that is causing something to happen.

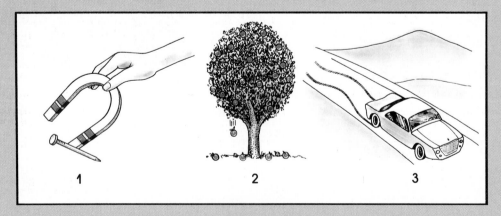

C. Write *T* for sentences that are true. Rewrite false sentences to make them true.

1. Force must be used to make things stop moving.
2. Objects with less mass are pulled more by gravity.
3. Friction is a force.
4. A lubricant is used to increase friction.
5. The ends of a magnet are called the north pole and the south pole.

USING IDEAS

1. On the moon, the pull of gravity is about one sixth of what it is on earth. Divide your weight by 6 to find out what you would weigh on the moon.
2. Make a bulletin board display showing objects being pushed or pulled by different forces.

THINKING LIKE A SCIENTIST

You may be able to answer some of these questions just by thinking about them. To answer other questions, you may have to do some research.

1. Explain how forces are different from matter.
2. Reducing friction on spacecraft can be a problem for scientists. In space, lubricants evaporate because of the heat from the sun. Why would this evaporation be a problem?
3. Steve held a very heavy package for 10 minutes. He did not know where to put it. Then Dan took the package from Steve and put it on a shelf. Which boy did work? Which boy did not do any work? Explain your answer.
4. Energy can change from one kind to another. Explain the energy changes in each of the following.
   a. Lightning strikes a tree and sets it on fire.
   b. The wind blows a door shut. The door slams with a loud bang.
   c. Someone strikes a match and uses it to light a candle.

Chapter 7

Machines

This girl is using a hammer to drive a nail into a piece of wood. She could not do this work using only her hands. So she is using a hammer. A hammer is a tool.

People use many other tools to help them with their work. All these tools are kinds of machines. Name some of the other machines in the picture. How can each be used to make work easier?

In this chapter you will learn about many different kinds of machines. You will also learn how machines help people with their work.

The Lever—A Simple Machine

How does a lever help do work?

People do many kinds of work each day. Sometimes they use machines when they work. A **machine** is something that helps people do work. Not all machines are the same. Some machines, like cars, have many moving parts. Other machines have few or no moving parts. They are called **simple machines.** A snow shovel is a simple machine. How is it different from a snowplow?

Using a snow shovel

Using a snowplow

Using a lever

A **lever** (lev'ər) is a simple machine. Levers are often used to lift or move things. These children are using a lever to move a heavy rock. To do this work, they must use force to push down on the tree branch. The object that will be moved, the rock, is called the **load.** The force and the load move in opposite directions.

As the lever moves the rock, it moves on a turning point. The turning point here is the log. Levers always use a force, a load, and a turning point when work is done.

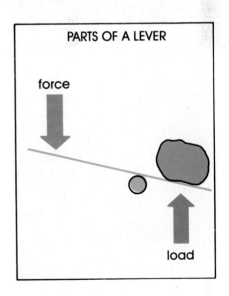

PARTS OF A LEVER

force

load

Riding a seesaw

Opening a jar

Pulling a nail

Have you ever ridden on a seesaw? If you have, then you have used a lever to lift someone. And that person used the same lever to lift you. Look at the first picture of the seesaw. Find the force, the load, and the turning point. Now look at the second picture. Did the force and the load change? How can you tell?

Not all levers look the same. Some are much shorter than a seesaw. This is a short lever. It is being used to open a jar. It would be hard to open the jar without using a lever like this.

This hammer is being used as a lever. It is being used to pull a nail out of wood. Where is the force coming from? What is the load? Do you think it would be easy to pull a nail without using a lever?

How does a lever work?

Materials   3 pencils / tape / wooden ruler / 2 small paper cups /small rock / paper clips

Procedure

A. Tape three pencils together.

B. Tape a small paper cup to each end of a wooden ruler.

C. Balance the ruler on the pencils.

D. Put a small rock into one of the cups.

E. Put paper clips, one at a time, into the other cup until the rock is lifted.
   1. How many paper clips were needed?

F. Empty both cups. Move one of the cups so that it is closer to the center of the ruler. Tape it. Put the small rock into this cup. Repeat step **E.**
   2. How many paper clips were needed to lift the rock?

Results
When the load is moved closer to the turning point, what happens to the amount of force needed?

Conclusion
1. What part of the lever is the turning point? What part is the load? What part is the force?
2. How does a lever work?

Using science ideas
How is the lever in this activity like the seesaw in the pictures on page 126?

127

Using an Inclined Plane

These people are using a ramp. A ramp makes it easier for them to put their things into the truck. A ramp is higher at one end than at the other. It is called an **inclined** (in klīnd') **plane.** An inclined plane is a simple machine. It can help in moving an object to a higher place.

Any slanted surface can be an inclined plane. A slanted board and a path going up a hill are both inclined planes. Some inclined

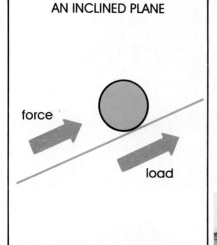

AN INCLINED PLANE

force

load

Using a ramp

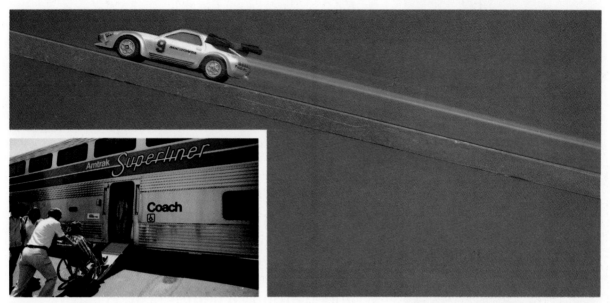

Different kinds of ramps

planes are very steep. Others are not. It takes more force to move up a steep inclined plane. In all inclined planes the force and the load move in the same direction.

Inclined planes are used in many places. Some are ramps for cars and trucks to use. Others are ramps for people to use. Maybe some of your toys have ramps. Think of other places where you have seen inclined planes.

Two inclined planes together make a simple machine called a **wedge** (wej). They come together to form a V-shaped edge. A wedge can be used to cut and split things apart. An ax is a wedge. Would you be able to split wood with the other side of an ax?

Ax and log

Turning a screw

Care should always be used with cutting tools.

Many other cutting tools are wedges. Nails and pins are also wedges. But they are very small. Can you name other wedges?

A **screw** is like an inclined plane that is wrapped around a center post. A screw must be turned to move into wood. Many jars have screw lids.

Finding Out

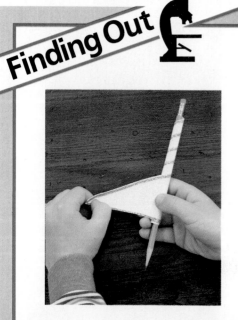

How is a screw like an inclined plane that is wrapped around a post?

Use a sheet of paper that measures about 12 centimeters by 24 centimeters. Draw a line from the upper left-hand corner to the lower right-hand corner. Use a ruler and a crayon. The line must be thick and straight. Now cut the paper along the line you have drawn. Does your paper look like an inclined plane? Place the paper triangle with the line on your desk. Lay it so that the line faces down. Line up your pencil with the shortest side of the triangle. Roll the paper tightly around the pencil. Now you know how a screw is like an inclined plane.

How does an inclined plane make work easier?

Materials 6 books / spring scale / string / small object / short board / long board

Moving the object	Amount of force needed
Lifting	
Pulling up on the short ramp	
Pulling up on the long ramp	

Procedure

A. Make a chart like the one shown. Write the answers to the questions below on your chart.

B. Pile 6 books, one on top of the other.

C. Use a piece of string to attach a small object to the hook on a spring scale.

D. Now use the spring scale to lift the object to the top of the pile of books. Read the spring scale.

   1. How much force was needed to lift the object?

E. Use a short board to make a ramp. Place the board between the top of the pile of books and the floor, as shown. Use the scale to pull the object up to the top of the ramp. Read the scale.

   2. How much force was needed to pull the object up the ramp?

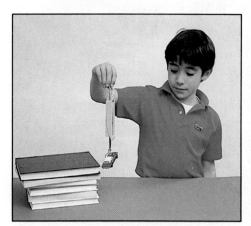

F. Now use a long board to make a ramp. Use the scale to pull the object up the ramp. Read the scale.

   3. How much force was needed to pull the object up the ramp?

Results

1. When was the most force needed to move the object?

2. When was the least force needed to move the object?

Conclusion

How does an inclined plane make work easier?

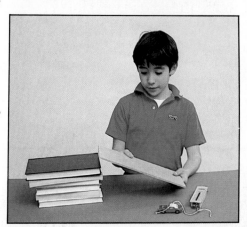

The Wheel and Axle

How does a wheel and axle help to make work easier?

There are many doors in your school and at home. You use a doorknob to open most of these doors. A doorknob is a simple machine called a wheel and axle (ak'səl). A **wheel and axle** is made of a wheel that turns on a center post. The center post is the axle. The wheel and axle makes it easier to turn and move things. Find the wheel and axle on the doorknob.

Turning a doorknob

Wheel-and-axle objects

There are many other examples of a wheel and axle. Sometimes a wheel and axle is easy to recognize. It is found on a bicycle, a wagon, and roller skates. All these things move on wheels. Name some other things that move on wheels.

Sometimes a wheel and axle is not so easy to recognize. Think of the steering wheel of a car. Here the axle is the steering column. A steering wheel allows a driver to turn the car. A driver does not have to use much force to do this. Less force is needed when the steering wheel is large. This is why many trucks have larger steering wheels than cars do. It would be hard for truck drivers to turn corners without large steering wheels.

Steering wheel and column

Fishing rod and reel

Turning a corner

A gear is a special kind of wheel and axle. A **gear** is a wheel with teeth. The teeth allow one gear to turn another. In the picture the large gear has more teeth than the smaller gear. The teeth of this large gear fit the teeth of the smaller gear. When the large gear turns, the smaller one does, too.

Gears are used in watches, cars, and many other machines. Here you can see the gears in an eggbeater. The beaters at the bottom turn faster than the handle. The gears in an eggbeater make it easier to mix things.

Using an eggbeater

gears inside a clock

Pulleys

When are pulleys used?

This man is raising flags on a pole. He could not do this job without using a simple machine called a pulley (pŭl'ē). A **pulley** is a wheel with a rope around it. The rope fits into a groove on the wheel. As the man pulls down on the rope, the flags are raised higher. The force and the load move in opposite directions.

Pulleys are used to move objects up, down, or sideways. They are also used to move objects, such as flags, to places that are hard to reach.

A FIXED PULLEY

load

force

Raising flags

Moving drapes

The pulley on the flagpole is called a fixed pulley. A **fixed pulley** stays in one place. Fixed pulleys are used to move some kinds of shades and drapes. Find the pulley that will be used to move the drapes.

Some pulleys are used to lift heavy loads. These pulleys move as the load is moved. They are called **movable pulleys.**

Usually a movable pulley is used together with a fixed pulley. The load is attached to the movable pulley. A single rope passes between both pulleys. When the rope is pulled, the load is raised. It is easy to move a heavy load in this way. Find a fixed pulley and a movable pulley in the picture.

Lifting a heavy load

Compound Machines

What are compound machines?

Many of the machines that people use are compound (kom'pound) machines. **Compound machines** are made of two or more simple machines. Scissors (siz'ərz) are made of two levers that work together. The cutting edges of scissors are shaped like wedges.

Cutting paper

Sharpening a pencil

Look at this pencil sharpener. The cover has been taken off. Which simple machines can you see? The handle is a wheel that turns on an axle. Another part of the sharpener looks like a screw. A compound machine like this one makes it fast and easy for you to sharpen a pencil. You probably use many other compound machines in school and at home.

Science & Technology

▶ Certain parts of the body work in much the same way as machines do. And like parts in machines, body parts can break or wear out. Now doctors are able to replace part of a bone in the hip. They are also able to replace the part of a knee that works like a hinge.

◀ The Jarvik-7 is a kind of artificial (är tə fish′əl) heart. It is used to replace a damaged heart. The Jarvik-7 can pump blood. Look in your library to learn more about the Jarvik-7.

Ideas to Remember

▶ Machines help people to do work.
▶ Simple machines have few or no moving parts.
▶ The lever, inclined plane, wheel and axle, and pulley are simple machines.
▶ Compound machines are made of two or more simple machines.

Reviewing the Chapter

SCIENCE WORDS

A. Copy the sentences below. Use science terms from the chapter to complete the sentences.

1. Machines having few or no moving parts are called _____.
2. A ramp, which is higher at one end than at the other, is called an _____.
3. A wheel with teeth is called a _____.
4. Two inclined planes together make a _____.
5. A _____ is a wheel with a rope around it.
6. A _____ is like an inclined plane that is wrapped around a center post.
7. A _____ is made of a wheel that turns on a center post.
8. A _____ always moves on a turning point.

B. Unscramble each group of letters to find a science term from the chapter. Write a sentence using each term.

1. munpodoc namiche
2. exdif lepluy
3. odal
4. emobavl lepluy
5. lepmis henicam
6. rocef

UNDERSTANDING IDEAS

A. Write T for sentences that are true. Rewrite false sentences to make them true.

1. A lever is a kind of compound machine.
2. Nails and pins are kinds of levers.
3. In all inclined planes, the force and the load move in the same direction.
4. A gear is a kind of wheel and axle.
5. When a fixed pulley is used, the force and the load move in opposite directions.

B. Name each of the simple machines pictured below. Explain how each helps to make work easier.

USING IDEAS

1. Invent a compound machine made of at least three simple machines. Draw a picture of your invention. Label the simple machines in the drawing.

2. List machines found in the classroom, on the playground, and at home. Make a bar graph showing the number of machines found in each of these places.

THINKING LIKE A SCIENTIST

You may be able to answer this question just by thinking about it, or you may have to do some research.

Which simple machines might you take with you if you were going on a camping trip? Make a list that gives as many examples as possible.

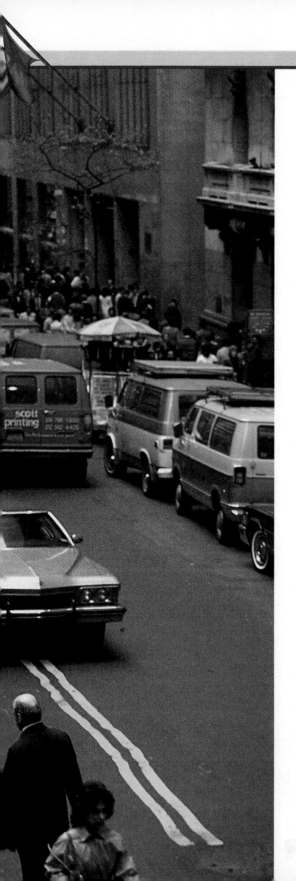

Chapter 8

Sound

Sounds are all around you. A busy
street in the middle of a city has many
kinds of sounds. Imagine you are
standing on the sidewalk at this place in
the city. What sounds would you hear?
How would the sounds be different?
What sounds would be unpleasant?
What sounds would be useful?

In this chapter you will learn about
sound. You will learn how sounds are
made and how they are different. You
will also learn how sound moves.

Making Sound

How is sound made?

Listen carefully to the sounds around you. Sound is a form of energy. Sound comes from matter that moves back and forth, or vibrates (vī'brāts). The back-and-forth movement is called **vibration** (vī brā'shən). A drum vibrates when it is hit. The ruler in one of the pictures is vibrating. What caused it to vibrate? Each of these objects makes sound when it vibrates.

You have learned that all matter is made of small particles. Sound moves through matter by making the particles vibrate. Without these particles of matter, sound could not move from place to place.

When a guitar string is plucked, it vibrates. The vibrating string makes the air particles around it move back and forth. These vibrating particles cause the particles next to them to vibrate. The vibration is passed from one particle to another. Soon particles far from the string are vibrating. In this way sound moves from place to place.

Sound moves in waves. The sound waves move through the air in every direction. The drawing shows how sound moves away from a ringing bell. People around the bell can hear the sound. It does not make any difference where they stand.

Plucked guitar string vibrating

Different Sounds

How are sounds different?

You know that sounds are different. There are loud sounds and there are soft sounds. The loudness or softness of a sound is called **volume** (vol′yəm). A loud sound has more volume than a soft sound. Look at the picture. If the drum is hit softly, the sound will be soft. If it is hit harder, the sound will be louder. The harder the drum is hit, the more it will vibrate. The air around the drum will also vibrate more, so the sound will be louder.

Making a kettledrum vibrate

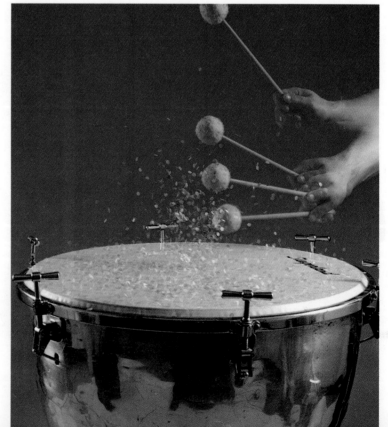

Another difference in sound is called pitch. **Pitch** is the highness or lowness of sound. Have you ever heard a tuba and a flute? They sound different. The tuba has a low pitch. The flute has a higher pitch.

The speed of vibrations controls the pitch. Fast vibrations make sounds that have a high pitch. Slow vibrations make sounds that have a low pitch. The flute makes air particles vibrate fast. The tuba makes air particles vibrate slowly.

Bands use instruments that make many kinds of sounds. The sounds are not the same even though the volume may be the same.

Playing a tuba

Some of the wind instruments in a band

Playing a flute

147

How can you make high sounds and low sounds?

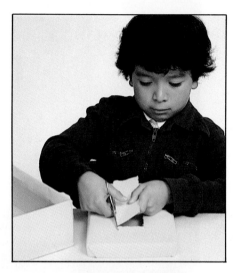

Materials   shoe box / scissors / 3 rubber bands of different thicknesses

Procedure

A. Remove the lid from a shoe box. Use the scissors to cut a rectangular opening in the lid, as shown in the picture. The opening should be about 15 centimeters long and 5 centimeters wide.

B. Place the lid onto the box. Place three rubber bands around the box. They should stretch over the opening. The rubber bands should be about 3 centimeters apart.
  1. How do you think the sound will be different if you lightly pluck each rubber band?

C. Lightly pluck each rubber band.
  2. How are the vibrations different?
  3. How are the sounds different?

Results
  1. Which rubber band has the highest pitch?
  2. Which rubber band has the lowest pitch?

Conclusion

What causes the difference in pitch among the rubber bands?

Using science ideas

1. How could you change this experiment to get different sounds?
2. Why does a violin or a guitar have strings of different thicknesses?

How Sound Moves

How does sound move through different kinds of matter?

Sound moves through all kinds of matter. You know it moves through air. Sound also moves through liquid and solid matter. In fact, sound moves differently through liquids and solids than through gases such as air.

The particles in gases are farther apart than those in liquids and solids. The distance between particles affects how well the particles can pass vibrations to each other. It is harder to send vibrations through matter when the particles are far apart. Since particles in air are farther apart, air does not carry vibrations as well as a liquid.

Science & Technology

◄ Did you know that there is a computer to help people who cannot speak? This computer has sounds in it. To make words, the person uses symbols that are on the keyboard. The sounds come out of a speaker.

▲ People who cannot hear well can wear a plastic bubble in their ear. The bubble has a tiny hole in it. This makes the sounds of other people's voices much louder.

SPEED OF SOUND

Type of matter	Speed (in meters per second)
Air	340
Water	1,500
Wood	3,500
Rock	3,700

Sound also moves through different matter at different speeds. Sound moves fastest through solids. It moves slowest through gases like air.

Look at the table. It shows the speed of sound through different kinds of matter. In what unit is speed measured? What is the speed of sound in air? What is the speed of sound in water? Why is the speed of sound through wood nearly the same as it is through rock?

Finding Out

How can you use sound to measure distance?

Light travels much faster than sound. Do you know that thunder and lightning happen almost at the same time? When lightning strikes, you see it instantly. But you often hear the thunder after you have seen the lightning. This is because sound moves at a much slower speed. The more time there is between seeing lightning and hearing thunder, the more distance there is between you and the storm.

You can measure the distance to a storm. Count how many seconds there are between lightning and thunder. Sound takes 3 seconds to move 1 kilometer. When you see lightning, count how many seconds it takes before you hear thunder. Divide the number of seconds by 3. The answer will be the distance in kilometers between you and the storm. How far away is lightning if it takes 12 seconds before you hear the thunder?

How does sound move through different kinds of matter?

Materials windup clock / metric ruler / self-sealing plastic bag / water

Procedure
A. Place a windup clock on a table. Use a metric ruler to measure a distance of 100 centimeters from the clock. Listen to the clock from that distance.
   1. Can you hear the clock through the air?

B. Measure 100 centimeters from the clock on the table. Place your ear on the table at this point. Listen to the clock.
   2. Can you hear the clock through the table?
   3. If you can hear the clock, how does it sound?

C. Fill a self-sealing plastic bag with water. Seal the bag and hold it against your ear. Have a classmate hold the clock against the bag of water.
   4. Can you hear the clock through the bag of water?
   5. If you can hear the clock, how does it sound?

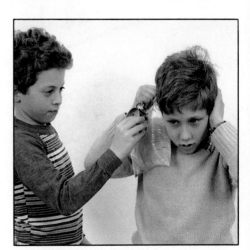

Conclusion
Does sound move best through a solid, a liquid, or a gas?

Using science ideas
Does sound move differently through some solids than it does through others? How could you find out?

How Sound Bounces

What happens when sounds strike different objects?

Sound moves all around us. It bounces off many surfaces. These sounds are reflected sounds. A **reflected sound** is one whose direction of movement has changed. A ball that is thrown against a wall bounces in another direction. Sounds that strike objects reflect, or bounce, in other directions, too.

The drawing shows how sound reflects from different surfaces. The sound that strikes a smooth surface reflects in one direction. The direction in which the sound reflects depends on how it strikes the surface. In what direction does sound reflect from a rough surface?

SOUND REFLECTION FROM
SMOOTH AND ROUGH SURFACES

How sound is reflected

Have you ever heard an echo (ek′ō)? An **echo** is a reflected sound. Echoes can be heard best in places where a hard surface is facing the source of sound.

Some surfaces absorb sound. They absorb sound like a sponge absorbs water. Sounds that are absorbed cannot bounce around.

Sound-absorbing material

Drapes absorb sound. Carpets and soft furniture also absorb sound. In which of these rooms would sound be absorbed better?

Finding Out

What is the best sound absorber?

Place a ticking alarm clock in a box. Make a small hole in the box. Place your ear near the hole. Listen to the sound of the ticking clock. Now use different materials to put around the clock. You can use wood, cloth, paper, and sponges. What other materials can you use? With each different material listen to the clock. Which one best absorbs the sound?

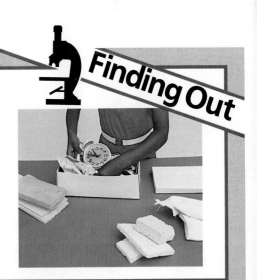

153

Sounds Made by Living Things

How do living things make sounds?

Sounds can be very interesting. Some of the most interesting sounds are made by animals. Animals and people use sounds to send messages to each other. The sending of these messages is called **communication** (kə myü nə kā'shən).

You communicate by sound when you talk. You talk by using the vocal (vō'kəl) cords in your throat. **Vocal cords** are special flaps of muscle that vibrate when you talk. The different vibrations of your vocal cords make different sounds. Your mouth and tongue help form these sounds.

vocal cords

Animals make sounds in many ways. Have you ever heard frogs and crickets at night? They make sounds in strange ways.

The spring peeper is a small frog with a big voice. You may have heard spring peepers singing at night. This frog fills a sac in its throat with air. The sac looks like a balloon. The frog uses the air in the sac to increase the volume of the sound it makes.

Crickets do not have vocal cords. They make sound by rapidly rubbing their wings together. This makes the air around them vibrate.

Cricket

Spring peeper

Some animals use sounds to locate objects. They produce sounds with a very high pitch. These sounds cannot be heard by people. Bats are animals that make such sounds. They give off sounds as they fly. These sounds reflect off objects, and the bat hears them echo. The bat uses the echo to find objects. Since bats do not see well, they use sound to find their way around when they fly. Dolphins also find objects by using sound in this way.

Sound is important to people as well as animals. But some people are deaf and cannot hear sound. They communicate with others by using special hand signals.

Dolphins

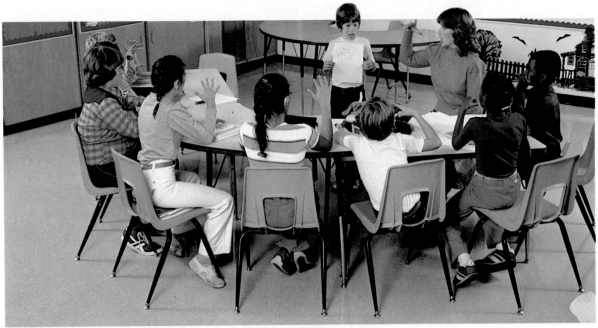
Teacher using hand signals to communicate with deaf children

Ideas to Remember

▶ Sound is a form of energy.
▶ Sound is produced when matter vibrates.
▶ Sound moves in waves in all directions from its source.
▶ The loudness or softness of a sound is called volume.
▶ Pitch is the highness or lowness of a sound.
▶ The speed of sound is fastest in solids and slowest in gases.
▶ An echo is a reflected sound.

Reviewing the Chapter

SCIENCE WORDS

A. Use all the terms below to complete the sentences.

pitch   vibration   reflected sound
        volume   matter

Sound comes from __1__ that moves back and forth. This back-and-forth movement is called __2__. Sound moves in waves in all directions. A __3__ is a sound that has changed the direction of its movement. The loudness or softness of a sound is called __4__. The highness or lowness of a sound is called __5__.

B. Write the letter of the term that best matches the definition. Not all the terms will be used.

1. The sending of messages from one to another
2. Produced when matter vibrates
3. Flaps of muscle that vibrate
4. Reflected sound
5. Highness or lowness of sound

a. vocal cords
b. echo
c. sound
d. volume
e. pitch
f. communication

UNDERSTANDING IDEAS

A. Write *T* for the sentences that are true. Rewrite false sentences to make them true.

1. Sound moves in waves in one direction from its source.
2. Sound is a form of energy.
3. The loudness or softness of sound is called pitch.
4. Slow vibrations make sounds that have a low pitch.
5. Rough surfaces reflect sound better than smooth surfaces.

B. Look at the drawing of a harp. Which strings would you pluck to get a high pitch? Explain your answer.

USING IDEAS

Make a list of all the sounds you can hear in your classroom. Next to each sound, write a description of it. Tell if the sound is pleasant or unpleasant, high or low, loud or soft. Discuss your list with other members of the class. Repeat this activity outdoors.

THINKING LIKE A SCIENTIST

You may be able to answer some of these questions just by thinking about them. To answer other questions, you may have to do some research.

1. Sometimes, breakfast cereals make popping sounds in milk. A popping balloon makes a similar sound. What causes these popping sounds?
2. Why does a guitar player have to keep tightening the strings on a guitar? Why is it necessary to have a piano tuned?
3. Why do people who are fishing ask children not to throw stones into the water?

4. Why are most auditoriums designed as this one is?

Science in Careers

Machines are important to everyone. People use machines in almost everything they do. **Mechanics** (mə kan'iks) tune and repair car engines.

Homemakers work with many kinds of machines. Machines make the homemaker's work easier. Some of the machines are simple, but most are compound.

Mechanic

Homemaker

Sound is also used in many ways. **Salespeople** tell about the things they sell. **Radio** and **TV reporters** talk about the news and the weather. A **disc jockey** uses recorded sound when playing records or tapes.

Disc jockey

People in Science

THOMAS EDISON
(1847–1931)

Thomas Edison was probably the world's greatest inventor. He is credited with more than 1,000 inventions. His inventions changed the lives of millions of people. Edison was interested in everything. But his greatest invention was the electric light bulb. He also invented the phonograph and a motion-picture machine, among other things.

Edison's phonograph

Developing Skills

WORD SKILLS

Many science words can be broken down into word parts. The tables list some word parts and their meanings.

Use the tables to find the meaning of some science words. You can do this by finding the meaning of each part of the word. For example, the word *telephone* is made of these parts: *tele + phone*.

1. telephone
2. telegraph
3. sonogram
4. megaphone
5. supersonic
6. graphic

Word part	Meaning
mega-	large
son-, sono-	sound
super-	above, over
tele-	far

Word part	Meaning
-gram	drawing
-graph	written
-ic	having to do with
-phone	sound

READING A TABLE

A table is a list of facts. Different kinds of sounds are listed in the table on the next page. The number next to each kind of sound tells how loud the sound is. The loudness of a sound is measured in units called decibels. The symbol for decibel is *dB*.

Use the table to answer the following questions.

1. Which sound is louder–city traffic or factory noise?

2. Which sound is softer–a subway train or a rock band?

3. Which sound is the loudest?

4. Which sound is twice as loud as a soft whisper?

5. Which sounds are not as loud as city traffic?

6. How much louder than a subway train is a rock band?

Kind of sound	Loudness (dB)
Soft whisper	30
Quiet in a library	40
Average home	50
Conversation	60
City traffic	70
Factory noise	80
Subway train	90
Rock band	110
Jet plane takeoff	140
Rocket launch	180

USING THINKING SKILLS

Pollution is anything in the air or water that makes it dirty or unsafe in some way. Some people call any loud sounds "noise pollution." Noise pollution can harm people just as air pollution can. Think about this as you answer the following questions.

1. What sounds might cause noise pollution?

2. Should people try to stop noise pollution? Explain your answer.

3. What are some ways to stop noise pollution?

Unit Three

Observing Our Earth and Its Neighbors

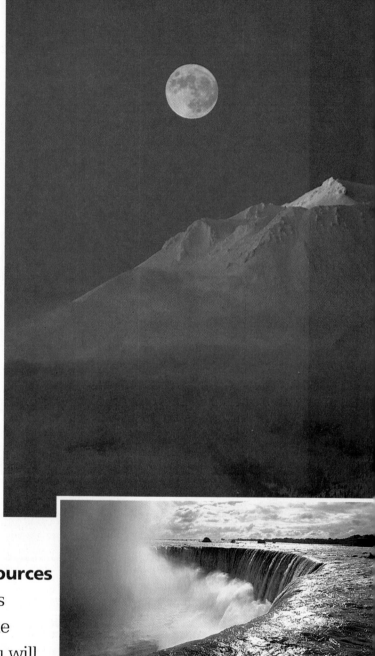

Chapter 9–The Changing Earth

Snow-covered mountains are found on some parts of the earth's surface. In this chapter you will find out how mountains change.

Chapter 10–The Earth's Resources

The water that flows over this waterfall may be used to make electricity. In this chapter you will learn about water and other useful things that come from the earth.

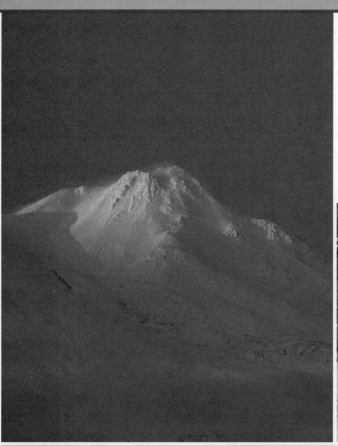

Chapter 11—The Weather Around You

During the winter season there may be many snowy days like this one. In this chapter you will find out what causes the seasons to change.

Chapter 12—Sun, Moon, and Planets

At sunset it looks to us as if the sun is moving down in the sky. But the sun does not move in this way. It is the earth that is moving.

Chapter 9

The Changing Earth

How old are you? How have you changed since last year? Perhaps you are taller now. People always change as they get older.

The earth changes, too, as it gets older. Some of these changes take a long time. They may take millions of years.

This picture shows a place that has been changing for a long time. The rock is being worn away. What do you think is causing this change? In this chapter you will learn about some ways the earth changes.

The Grand Canyon

Inside the Earth

What is it like inside the earth?

In some ways, the earth can be compared to a hard-boiled egg. Look at the drawings of the earth and the egg cut in half. How are they alike? You can see that they both have three layers.

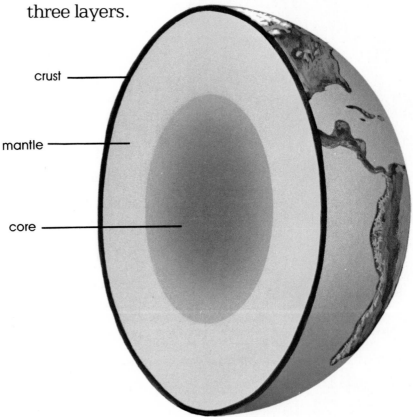

crust

mantle

core

The outer layer of the earth is called the **crust** (krust). Like the eggshell, the crust is the thinnest layer. The crust is made mostly of solid rock. The crust is the most important layer of the earth. You live on the crust.

Using land for farming

Rock outcrop

Food is grown in soil that is part of the crust. Many important materials come from within the crust. Some of these materials are coal, oil, and iron.

Under the earth's crust there is a thicker layer of rocklike material. This layer is called the **mantle** (man'təl). Scientists have never dug into the mantle. But they know it is hot.

The layer beneath the mantle is called the **core** (kôr). Scientists do not think the core is made of rock. They think it is mostly iron. The outer part of the core may be liquid. The center of the core may be solid. The core is the hottest part of the earth.

How can you tell what is inside something without looking?

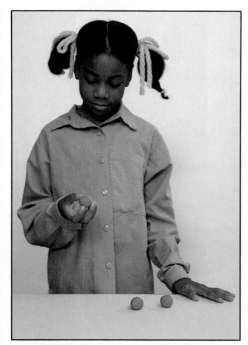

Materials   3 clay balls / toothpick / compass

Procedure

A. Examine the outside of three clay balls. Each ball may contain a rock, a marble, a metal screw, a piece of wood, a piece of paper, or nothing.

   1. What do you think is inside each ball?

B. Try to find out if there is an object inside each ball. To do this, you may poke a toothpick 15 times into each ball. Be careful not to change the shape of the ball.

   2. Did you find an object in each ball?

   3. What do you think the size and shape of each object may be?

C. A compass needle is a magnet. Find out if anything inside each ball moves the needle in a compass.

   4. Did any of the objects move the compass needle?

   5. If so, what must the object be made of?

D. Try to guess what is inside each ball.

E. Break apart each ball and look inside.

Conclusion

1. Were you able to find out what was in each ball without looking inside?

2. What else could you have done to find out about the objects?

Using science ideas

How do you think scientists get ideas about what is inside the earth?

Fast Changes in the Crust

How do earthquakes and volcanoes change the earth's crust?

The earth's crust is always changing. Some changes are very fast. They may take only a few minutes.

Earthquakes (ẻrth'kwāks) cause fast changes in the earth's crust. An **earthquake** is a movement of rock in the crust. This may happen when forces inside the earth push up on the crust. Land may rise or fall when layers of the crust crack and move. Sometimes this movement causes damage at the surface of the crust.

MOVEMENT OF ROCK LAYERS

Earthquake damage

Science & Technology

▲ Before an earthquake, there are movements of rock inside the earth. People cannot feel these movements. But they are felt by a seismograph (sīz′ mə graf). When this machine draws wavy lines, it means that there may be an earthquake.

▲ Scientists will soon send this satellite (sat′ ə līt) into space. From there it will be able to identify places on the earth's surface that have moved.

Scientists are always looking for better ways to predict earthquakes. What are some reasons why this is important?

It is very hot deep inside the earth's crust. It is hot enough to melt rock. Melted rock is called **magma** (mag′mə). The magma may move up through cracks in the earth's crust. As more and more magma is pushed up to the surface, a volcano (vol kā′nō) is formed. A **volcano** is an opening in the earth's crust through which magma flows.

Here you can see how hot melted rock flows from a volcano. Melted rock that flows from a volcano is called **lava** (lä′və). After lava cools, it hardens into solid rock.

INSIDE A VOLCANO

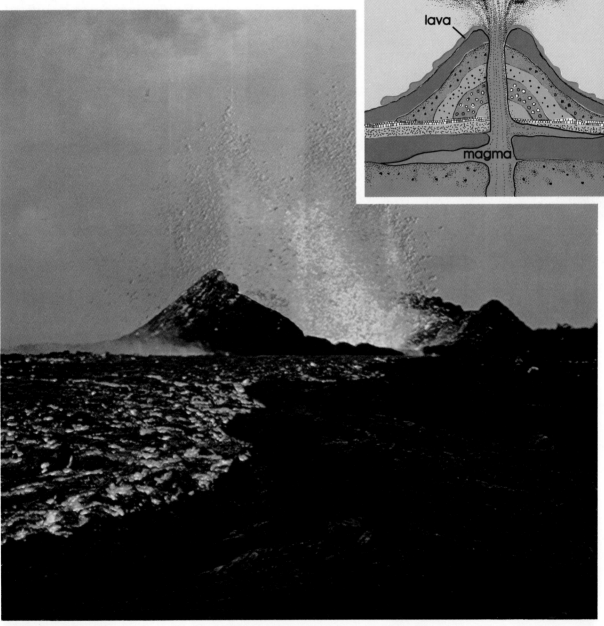

An active volcano

Slower Changes in the Crust

How are the rocks in the earth's crust changing?

Most people think that anything made of rock will last forever. Rocks may not seem to change. But the rocks on the earth's surface are always changing. Some are slowly worn away. Others are broken into smaller pieces. The wearing away and breaking of rock is called **weathering** (weŦH′ər ing). Most weathering is done by moving water and wind.

Weathered rocks

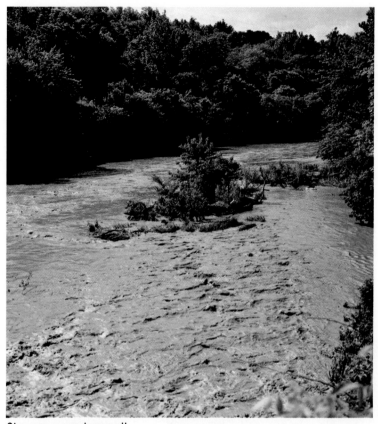
Stream carrying soil

What happens after rocks are broken into smaller pieces? Some pieces of rock may become part of the soil. Water or wind may carry other pieces to new places. The movement of rock and soil by water and wind is called **erosion** (i rō′zhən).

These pictures show what erosion can do. The stream looks muddy. Soil is being carried to a new place. You can also see land that has been changed by erosion. How will this land look if there is any more erosion?

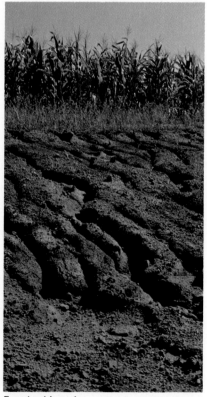
Eroded land

Changes Caused by Water

How does water change the earth's crust?

Have you ever seen the rocks near a river or stream? Most of them are round and smooth. What causes these rocks to become round and smooth?

Fast-moving water in a river or stream can move rocks. The rocks bump into and roll over each other. This causes the sharp edges to break off. In time, the rocks are worn smooth. The water has weathered the rocks.

Rounded rocks

Fast-moving water carries pieces of rock and soil with it. These rocks and soil change the bottom of the river or stream. They cut into it and make it deeper. When the water slows, rocks and soil settle to the bottom. After many years, layers of rock and soil will form new land. Look at the picture. Find the new land that has been formed here.

New land

Water changes rocks in other ways. Sometimes water gets into small holes and cracks in rocks. In cold weather the water can freeze. Water expands as it freezes. Freezing water will make the cracks wider. Soon the rock will start to break into smaller pieces. Freezing water in the cracks of rocks is another way rocks are weathered.

Cracked rocks

Activity

How does weathering change rocks?

Materials rock salt / hand lens / sand / small jar with lid / spoon / water / shallow dish /paper

Procedure

A. Place a few pieces of rock salt on a sheet of paper. Look at the rock salt through a hand lens. Draw what you see.

    1. Describe the size and shape of the pieces of rock salt.

B. Put enough rock salt into a jar to cover the bottom. Add a spoonful of sand. Cover the salt and sand with water. Put a lid on the jar.

C. Shake the covered jar for 2 minutes.

    2. What do you think is happening to the rock salt?

D. Remove the lid from the jar. Pour the water into a dish. Empty the pieces of rock salt onto the sheet of paper.

E. Look at the rock salt through the hand lens.

    3. How have the size and shape of the pieces of rock salt changed?

Results

How did weathering change the rock salt?

Conclusion

How can moving water and sand in a river or stream change rocks?

Changes Caused by Wind

How does strong wind change the earth's crust?

Have you ever had dust blown in your face? This may happen on a windy day. Wind may carry pieces of sand and soil.

A dust storm

This picture shows what a dust storm is like. You can see sand and soil being picked up by the wind. Strong winds may blow sand and soil far from where they have been formed. When the winds slow down, these materials are dropped. Sand dunes like these may form. Strong winds cause much weathering and erosion.

Sand dunes

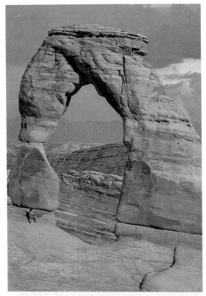

An arch of rock

Sand carried by strong winds can wear away rocks. The moving sand hits the rock. It grinds away bits of the rock. In time the shape of the rock changes. These rocks have been carved by winds that carry pieces of sand.

Sometimes land must be protected from wind. Strong winds may carry away soil that is needed. Land covered with plants will slow down this kind of erosion. The roots of plants hold soil in place.

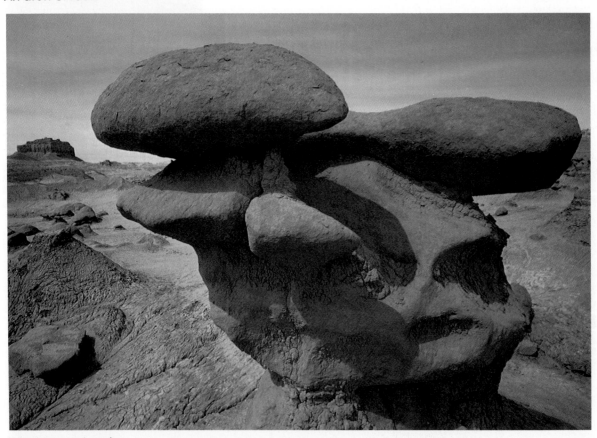

Wind-carved rocks

Changes Caused by Living Things

How do living things change the crust?

People, plants, and animals live on the earth's crust. Sometimes they change parts of the crust. Perhaps even you have changed some of the crust.

People need roads. The land must be changed when roads are built. Large rocks are broken and moved.

A mountain highway

Digging a foundation

Can you find signs of weathering and erosion?

Look in your yard or neighborhood. Buildings, roads, and sidewalks often show signs of weathering. Look for examples of erosion. You may find places where wind or water is carrying soil or sand away.

Make a chart like this one. It will help you to remember what you have seen. On the chart tell if you have seen weathering or erosion. Tell where it is and what caused it. You may want to make some drawings of what you have seen.

Cracked sidewalk

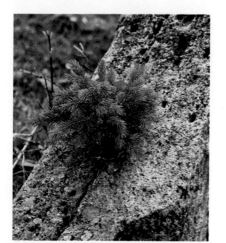
Tree growing in rock

You may have seen how a tree root can lift and crack a sidewalk. Growing plants can change rocks in the same way. The roots of some plants start to grow in cracks in rocks. As the roots get bigger, the rocks crack more and more. What will happen to this rock as the tree grows?

Some animals move soil and rocks to look for food. They may even live in the soil.

A badger digging

Ideas to Remember

▶ The layers of the earth are the crust, the mantle, and the core.

▶ The crust is always changing.

▶ Earthquakes and volcanoes cause fast changes in the earth's crust.

▶ Weathering and erosion cause slower changes in the earth's crust.

▶ The crust is changed by water, wind, and living things.

Reviewing the Chapter

SCIENCE WORDS

A. Copy the sentences below. Use science terms from the chapter to complete the sentences.

1. The wearing away and breaking of rock is called ____.
2. The outer layer of the earth is called the ____.
3. Melted rock inside the earth is called ____.
4. An ____ is a movement of rock in the earth's crust.
5. The movement of rock and soil by water and wind is called ____.
6. The ____ is the hottest part of the earth.
7. A ____ is an opening in the earth's crust through which melted rock flows.
8. The ____ is a layer of rocklike material under the earth's crust.
9. Melted rock that flows from a volcano is called ____.

B. Write as many science terms from the chapter as you can, using the letters in the box. The same letter may be used more than once. Write a sentence using each term.

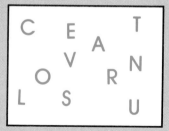

UNDERSTANDING IDEAS

A. Write sentences that tell how each of these makes the earth's crust change.

1. earthquake   2. volcano   3. water   4. wind
5. plants   6. animals   7. people

B. Write the term that does not belong in each group.

1. crust, mantle, plant, core
2. lava, wind, magma, volcano
3. wind, core, water, living things
4. weathering, erosion, earthquake, soil

C. The drawings show some changes in the earth's crust. Write the numbers of the pictures. Next to each number write the cause of the change.

USING IDEAS

The earth's crust is changed by water, wind, and living things. Write about two ways in which you have changed the earth's crust.

THINKING LIKE A SCIENTIST

You may be able to answer some of these questions just by thinking about them. To answer other questions, you may have to do some research.

1. You are given a hot roll to eat. It is too hot to bite into. After you wait for a few minutes, the outside of the roll becomes cooler and harder. You bite into the roll. It is still so hot that steam comes from the inside. In what ways is the roll like the earth?

2. Scientists try to predict exactly when earthquakes will occur. What science facts might be important in predicting earthquakes? Why are these facts important? Why is this type of scientific work important?

3. In the spring heavy rains cause the erosion of topsoil in vegetable gardens. This is a problem. In the summer this is not such a big problem. Why is there more erosion in the spring than there is in the summer?

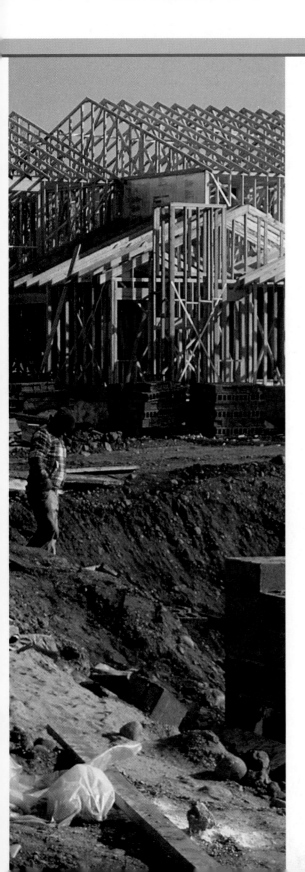

Chapter 10

The Earth's Resources

Have you ever watched a house being built? If you have, you know that many materials are needed.

In this picture you can see the workers using many different materials. In some way, all of these materials once came from the earth. Name some of the things that came from the earth. Where did the cinder blocks come from? Where did the wood come from?

In this chapter you will learn about many useful things that come from the earth.

Soil as a Resource

Why do plants and animals need soil?

Many of the things you need for life come from the earth. You could not live without soil, air, and water. Useful materials from the earth are called **natural resources** (nach′ər əl ri sôr′siz). Soil, air, and water are natural resources.

Soil is a very important natural resource. Plants need soil to grow. People use many kinds of plants for food. People use trees for lumber and to make paper. Every day you use many things that were grown in soil. How many things have you used today that were grown in soil?

Redwood trees

Redwood lumber

Soil is made of many kinds of matter. Most soil is made of pieces of weathered rock. The rock pieces may be very large or as fine as powder.

Most soil has matter that was once living. The remains of dead plants and animals have become part of the soil. When this happens, many useful materials are returned to the soil. Plant and animal matter found in soil is called **humus** (hyü′məs).

Topsoil

Humus is found in the top layer of soil. This layer of soil is called **topsoil.** Humus helps topsoil to hold water. Plants grow well in topsoil that has a lot of humus.

Sometimes worms live in the soil. Worms use humus for food. Worms make tunnels in the soil. The tunnels allow air and water to move through the soil. Plants need this air and water to grow.

Activity

How are two kinds of soil different from each other?

Materials 2 paper towels / 2 soil samples / hand lens / 2 small jars with lids / masking tape / pencil / water

Procedure

A. Place two paper towels on your desk. Label one towel *A* and the other towel *B*. Put a sample of soil on each towel.

B. Look at each sample.
   1. How are the two soils alike?
   2. How are the two soils different?

C. Make a chart like the one shown.

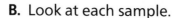

Material in soil	Sample A	Sample B
Large rock particles		
Small rock particles		
Plant remains		
Animal remains		

D. Use a hand lens to look for different materials in each sample. Write *yes* or *no* on your chart to answer the following questions.
   3. Which soil has large rock particles?
   4. Which soil has small rock particles?
   5. Which soil has plant and animal remains?

E. Use masking tape to label one jar *A* and the other jar *B*.

F. Put soil sample *A* into jar *A*. Put soil sample *B* into jar *B*. Pour water into the jars so that they are nearly full. Put the lids on tightly. Shake each jar to mix the water and the soil. Wait for the soil in each jar to settle.
   6. What happened to the soil in each jar?

Conclusion
Explain how the two kinds of soil are different from each other.

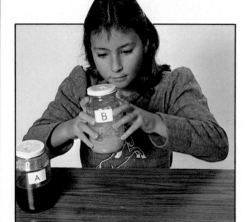

The Air Around Us

Why is air an important natural resource?

There is air all around you. But you cannot see it. Pure air has no color. You cannot smell pure air. Sometimes you can feel air when it moves. Moving air is called wind. Wind has energy that can make things move. This energy can be used to turn windmills and move sailboats. How else can wind be used?

Windmill

Sailboats

Air is made of many different gases. A gas called nitrogen (ni′trə jən) makes up most of the air. Oxygen (ok′sə jən) is another important gas in the air. Most living things need oxygen. There are also small amounts of other gases in the air.

TECHNOLOGY

◄ Wind power is useful. Hundreds of years ago, wind power was used to pump water. Wind power was also used to grind wheat into flour.

► Today, wind power has a new use. It is being used to produce electricity. First, wind turns the blades of a windmill. The blades then turn a machine called a generator (jen′e rā ter). This is what produces electricity.

▼ Wind turbines (ter′binz) are the modern windmills that drive generators to produce electricity. Some turbines are between 10 and 15 stories high. They may have two long blades or many tall blades.

Wind could be an important source of power in the future. It is free. And wind does not pollute anything. Think of some other reasons why wind is a good energy source.

Pollution from a car

The air around the earth is called the **atmosphere** (at′mə sfir). The atmosphere is not always clean. Winds blow soil into the air. Volcanoes put dust into the air. Many factories put smoke into the air. Cars and trucks add harmful gases to the air.

Anything that makes the air dirty causes **pollution** (pə lü′shən). Air pollution harms many living things. People can become sick from air pollution.

Today many things are being done to control air pollution. Perhaps you can tell what some of these things are.

Mount St. Helens

How can you find out where there is air pollution?

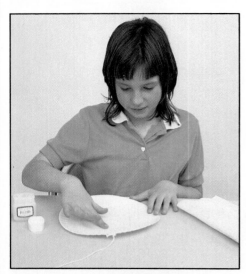

Materials white paper plate that is coated / string, 30 cm long /paper clip / petroleum jelly / hand lens

Procedure

A. Make an air pollution collector. To do this, make a small hole near the edge of a paper plate. Tie one end of a piece of string through the hole. Tie a paper clip to the other end of the string.

B. Your teacher will give you a number to write on the back of your plate.

C. Carefully spread a thin layer of petroleum jelly on the center of the plate.

D. Take your plate to a place where you think the air is dusty. Carefully hang the plate in that place.

   1. Where did you hang your plate?

E. After 3 days, bring the plate back to the classroom. Be careful not to touch the center of the plate.

F. Use a hand lens to look at the center of the plate.

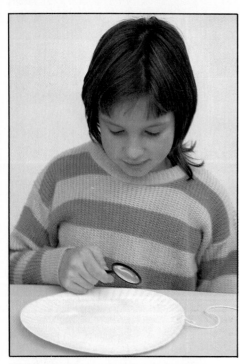

Results

Describe what you see on the plate.

Conclusion

In which places did you find air pollution?

Using science ideas

Think of some things that people can do to keep the air clean.

The Earth's Water Supply

Where can water be found on the earth?

Much of the earth is covered with water. Water is found in oceans, rivers, lakes, and ponds. There may be water in the ground. In some places, water is even found as large pieces of ice. Wherever it is found, water is an important natural resource.

Large iceberg

Shasta Dam and its reservoir

Irrigation

The water that people use comes from many different places. Where there are many people, the water may come from a reservoir (rez′ər vwär). A **reservoir** is a place where water is stored.

Water is needed for farm crops. Most crops get enough water from rain. But in some places there is not enough rain for crops to grow. Farmers must give water to these plants. Giving water to crops when there is not enough rain is called **irrigation** (ir ə gā′shən).

Living things always need water. But sometimes water becomes polluted. This happens when wastes from factories and houses get into the water. Polluted water can harm living things.

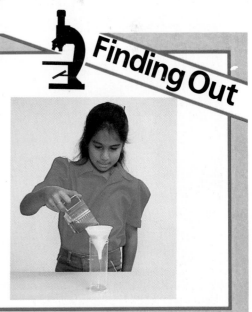
Removing oil from a duck

Cleaning an oil spill

Finding Out

How can you clean water?

Water from reservoirs must be cleaned before it can be used. Water is cleaned in several steps. In one step the water passes through a filter.

You can make a filter out of a funnel. Put a large wad of cotton into the bottom of a funnel. Then cover the cotton with a layer of clean sand. Hold the funnel over a glass to collect the water as it is filtered. Slowly pour some muddy water into the funnel. Watch as the filtered water drips into the jar. What happens to the muddy water as it is filtered?

Energy from the Earth

What kinds of energy come from the earth's crust?

Using gas to cook

Every day you need energy to do many things. You need energy to do work and to play. Your energy comes from the food you eat. Your body uses food as a fuel. A **fuel** is a material that is used to supply energy.

People need many other kinds of energy. Energy is needed to heat homes and to cook food. Energy is needed to move trucks and to run machines.

Fueling a truck

Coal mining and coal

Oil rig and pump

Many fuels are buried in the layers of the earth's crust. Coal, oil, and gas are important fuels that come from the earth's crust. They all give off energy when they are burned. Here you can see how coal is taken from the earth. Oil and gas must be pumped to the surface of the earth.

It took millions of years for coal, oil, and gas to form. These fuels formed from the remains of plants and animals that lived long ago. Fuels are important natural resources.

199

Some Other Resources

Why are some rocks useful?

You may not think that rocks are useful. But some rocks are. Metals such as iron, copper, gold, and silver are found in rocks. These metals are mixed with other minerals. Rocks that contain metals are called **ores** (ôrz). Mines like this one have been dug to take ores from the earth's crust.

Most of the metals people use come from ores. Coins are made of metal. Most tools and machines are also made of metals.

A copper mine and copper ore

Some rocks are useful because they are strong and beautiful. One of these rocks is marble (mär′bəl). Marble has been used in many buildings.

Lyndon B. Johnson Library

Marble quarry

Sometimes beautiful minerals are found in rocks. These minerals are called **gems** (jemz). Most gems are used to make jewelry. Diamonds (dī′məndz) are one kind of gem.

Ideas to Remember

▶ Natural resources are useful materials that come from the earth.

▶ Living things need soil, air, and water for life.

▶ Coal, oil, and gas are used for energy.

▶ Soil, air, water, fuels, metals, and gems are natural resources.

Diamond

Reviewing the Chapter

SCIENCE WORDS

A. Copy the sentences below. Use science terms from the chapter to complete the sentences.

1. Useful materials from the earth are called _____.
2. Plants grow well in soil that has a lot of _____.
3. The air around the earth is called the _____.
4. A gas called _____ makes up most of the air.
5. Most living things need a gas called _____ from the air.
6. Sometimes the water that people use is stored in a _____.
7. Anything that makes air or water dirty causes _____.
8. Watering crops when there is not enough rain is called _____.

B. Find the missing letters for each term. Write a sentence using each term.

1. g _ _ s   2. _ u e _   3. _ r _ s   4. t o _ s _ i l

UNDERSTANDING IDEAS

A. A *cause* makes things happen. An *effect* is what happens. For each pair of sentences, tell which is the cause and which is the effect.

1. **a.** The air in the atmosphere is not always clean.
   b. Cars and trucks add harmful gases to the air.
2. **a.** Wind has energy that makes things move.
   b. Sailboats move down the river.
3. **a.** Some rocks are used in buildings.
   b. Some rocks are strong and beautiful.
4. **a.** The earth has many natural resources.
   b. Plants and animals can live on earth.

B. Write sentences telling how each of these natural resources is used by people.

1. soil   **2.** water   **3.** metal   **4.** oil   **5.** air   **6.** gas

USING IDEAS

Look at old magazines and newspapers. Cut out pictures that show how natural resources are used. Put the pictures into groups for each kind of natural resource. Make a poster to show your pictures.

THINKING LIKE A SCIENTIST

You may be able to answer some of these questions just by thinking about them. To answer other questions, you may have to do some research.

1. Scientists often use models to help explain their ideas. The models make the ideas easier to understand. Models can also help to describe things. How, then, is the rind of an orange like the earth and its atmosphere?

2. Why do garden supply stores sell potting soil? How do you think this soil differs from regular soil?

3. Sometimes, dams must be opened to allow water to escape from reservoirs. What problem does releasing the water solve?

Chapter 11

The Weather Around You

The weather around you changes from day to day. You may wake up to see the sun shining through your bedroom window. By the time you come home from school it may be raining.

The weather changes in many ways. It can change from warm to cold. It can change from calm to windy. How is the weather in the picture about to change?

In this chapter you will learn about the weather and its changes. You will also learn about what causes the weather to change.

Heating the Earth

How is the earth heated?

You can see that the ice statue is melting even though it is a cold day. It is melting because it is in the sunlight. Have you ever stood in the sun and felt the heat? How do you feel when you walk out of the sunlight and into the shade?

Ice statue

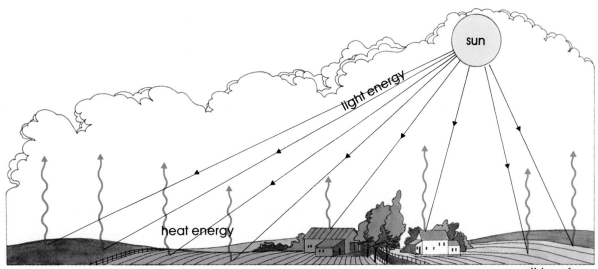

light energy

heat energy

earth's surface

You know that the sun gives off light energy. Some of the light energy travels through space and reaches the earth. When light energy strikes the earth, some of it is changed to heat. The drawing will help you understand how this happens. Have you ever walked barefoot on a beach on a sunny day? If you have, you know the sand felt warm. How did the sand get warm?

The earth is like a giant heater. Heat coming from the earth's surface warms the air above the land. The temperature of the air changes with the amount of sunlight that reaches the earth's surface. The more sunlight the surface gets, the more the air is heated. Why is the air cooler on a cloudy day? Why does it get cooler at night?

Stepping on warm sand

Seasons

What causes the temperature to change with the seasons?

The temperature of many parts of the earth changes with the seasons. These changes are caused by the way light from the sun strikes the earth. Light from the sun strikes the earth differently in winter than it does in summer. Look at the drawings. You can see that during winter, sunlight strikes the earth at a slant. Light striking at a slant spreads out. The ground in this area is heated less at this time of year. In summer, sunlight strikes the earth more directly. This light does not spread out. So the ground gets more heat with direct sunlight.

SUMMER

WINTER

The tilt of the earth as it moves around the sun causes the change in seasons. Look at the drawing. In summer, the part of the earth where you live is tilted toward the sun. The sunlight strikes the surface more directly. In winter, your part of the earth tilts away from the sun. How does sunlight strike the earth in the winter?

Did you ever notice how much longer the days are in summer than in winter? In winter you may get up when it is still dark outside. In summer you might wake up with the sun in your eyes. There are more hours of daylight in summer than there are in winter. More hours of daylight also cause the earth to become warmer in summer.

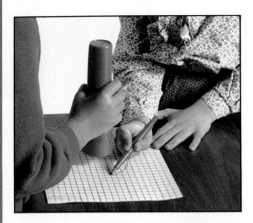

Activity

How are direct rays of light and slanting rays of light different?

Materials   flashlight / pencil / graph paper

Procedure

A. Hold a flashlight 2 centimeters above a sheet of graph paper. Draw a line around the edge of the outer ring of light.

   1. How many full squares can you count inside the circle?

B. Hold the flashlight at a slant 2 centimeters above the paper. Draw a line around the outer ring of light.

   2. How many full squares can you count inside the circle?

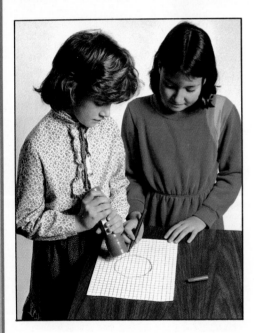

Results

1. What is the difference between the number of squares counted in step **A** and in step **B**?
2. Did the amount of light change from step **A** to step **B**?
3. Did the amount of space lighted by the flashlight change from step **A** to step **B**?
4. Did each square in step **A** receive more or less light than each square in step **B**?

Conclusion

How are direct rays of light and slanting rays of light different?

Using science ideas

At what times during the day do you think the sun would heat the earth's surface the least? Why?

210

Heating Different Surfaces

What part of the earth absorbs the most sunlight?

Some energy from the sun changes to heat when it strikes the surface of the earth. The surface of the earth is not the same in all places. Three fourths of the earth is covered by water. The rest of the earth is land. The land changes sunlight to heat faster than the water does. This causes the air over water to be cooler than the air over land during the day.

Light-colored surfaces do not absorb light as well as dark surfaces. When the sun's light strikes light-colored surfaces, much of it bounces off. This light is not changed to heat. The cars in the picture are sitting in the sun. Suppose you could touch each car. Which ones would feel warmest?

Land and water

Light and dark-colored cars

Fields

Many polar regions are covered with snow. Why is the air in these regions cold? Since dark surfaces can absorb more light, they become warmer than light-colored surfaces. The air above dark surfaces also becomes warmer. Which fields in the picture give off the most heat on a sunny day? Why?

Differences in temperature can cause air to move. Warm air is lighter than cold air. Warm air rises when cooler, heavier air moves in and pushes it upward. You can see this happening in the drawing below. Moving air is called **wind.** Wind helps bring many of the changes in weather.

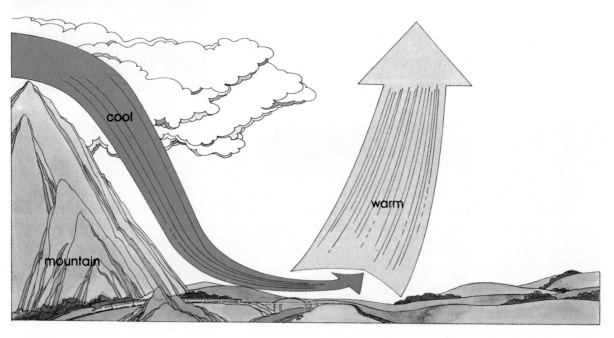

Water in the Air

How is water changed to a gas?

Energy from the sun does more than heat the earth. It also changes water in lakes, rivers, and oceans. The water is changed to a gas by evaporation. Water in the form of a gas is called water vapor. The particles of water vapor are very small. They are so small that you cannot see them in the air.

Water evaporates faster at some times than at other times. What happens to puddles of water when the sun shines? Will the clothes on the line dry faster if the wind is blowing? Both wind and heat from sunlight speed up the evaporation of water.

Drying clothes

Puddle of water

Water vapor in the air can change back to liquid water. Have you ever seen water on the grass in the morning? This water is called **dew.** It forms when the air and grass become cool. The water vapor in the air changes back to liquid when it touches the cool grass.

Sometimes the temperature of the air drops below freezing. When the air is colder than 0°C, small ice crystals form on the grass. Ice formed in this way is called **frost.** Where else have you seen frost?

Frost

Dew

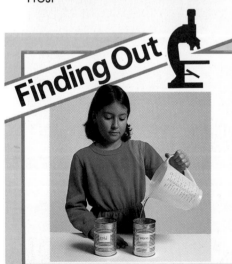

Is there water vapor in the air around you?

Fill a tin can with ice cubes and cold water. Fill another can with warm water. Make sure the water comes to the same level in both cans. Wait 15 minutes. Wipe a finger across the outside of each can. What do you notice? Where does the water come from?

Clouds

What happens to water in the clouds?

Warm, moist air gets cooler as it rises. As the air cools, the particles in the air move closer together. When this happens, water vapor is squeezed from the spaces between the air particles. This causes the water vapor to form tiny drops of water on bits of dust. The tiny drops of water are so light that they float in the air. When millions of these drops come together, they form a **cloud.**

There are many kinds of clouds. Some form high in the sky. Others form lower in the sky. The drawing shows three kinds of clouds and where they form.

high clouds (feathery)

middle clouds (fluffy)

low clouds (layered)

Fog

Some clouds are very thick and form in layers. There must be a lot of water vapor in the air for these clouds to form. Other clouds form very high above the ground, where there is not much water vapor in the air. It is below freezing where these clouds form. These clouds are thin. They are made of ice crystals.

Have you ever walked in a cloud? If you have walked in a fog, you have walked in a cloud. Fog is a cloud close to the ground.

Sometimes clouds gather into thick layers. The wind blows the clouds into cooler air. The drawing shows what happens inside a cloud when the cloud meets cooler air. (1) Small drops of water in clouds come closer together. (2) The small drops join to make larger and heavier drops. (3) The drops become so heavy that they cannot float in the air. They fall to the ground as rain.

Sometimes the temperature of the air below a cloud is very cold. The rain freezes as it falls. Frozen raindrops are called **sleet.**

During winter the temperature in the clouds may be below freezing. Water vapor in the clouds freezes into tiny crystals of ice. **Snowflakes** form when more water vapor freezes onto the ice crystals. In time the snowflakes fall from the cloud. Snowflakes can be seen in many different shapes. How are the snowflakes in the pictures different? Snow, rain, and sleet are called **precipitation** (pri sip ə tā'shən).

Snowflakes

Science & Technology

Have you ever wished you could do something to change the weather? People have been trying to do this for many years.
▶ Sometimes there is not enough rain. To make it rain, scientists use something called cloud seeding. To do this, dry ice is dropped from airplanes into rain clouds. Or a chemical called silver iodide (i´ ə dīd) is put into the clouds. In the picture, the kite contains silver iodide. Think of reasons why cloud seeding may or may not be a good idea.

Water Cycle

What are the steps of the water cycle?

Do you know that water is always moving around you? It is evaporating from bodies of water such as rivers, streams, and oceans. This water rises and cools to form clouds. When clouds cool, tiny drops of water join together and fall to the ground.

One of three things happens to water that falls onto land as rain or snow. (1) Most of it soaks into the ground. (2) Some of it evaporates into the air. (3) Some of it flows into rivers and streams. In time the water in rivers and streams will reach large lakes and oceans. This water evaporates once again into the air. Most of the earth's surface is covered by ocean water. For this reason, most water evaporates from oceans.

The moving of water from the oceans to the air and back to the oceans is called a **water cycle** (sī′kəl). A cycle is something that happens over and over again. A cycle always leads back to where it started. The seasons of the year are another kind of cycle. They happen over and over again. What other cycles can you name?

After a rainstorm

The drawing will help you understand the water cycle. Look at each numbered step as you read.

(1) Energy from the sun changes water to water vapor. (2) Water vapor rises, cools, and condenses to form clouds. (3) Winds blow the clouds over land. (4) Clouds meet cool air, and rain or snow falls to the ground. (5) Most of the water returns to the oceans. The water that returns can now begin the cycle once again.

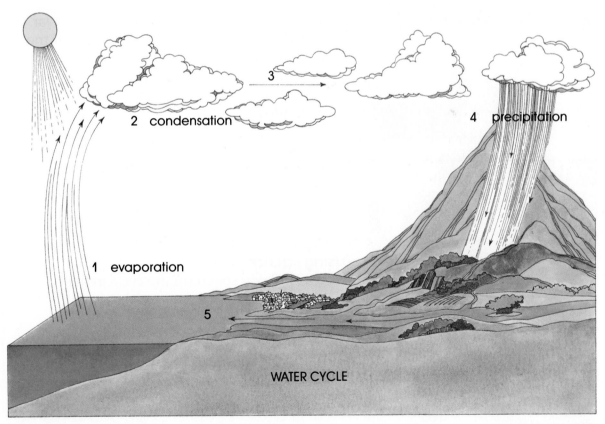

WATER CYCLE

How can you make a water cycle?

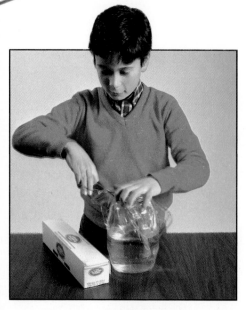

Materials   large jar / plastic wrap / rubber band / water

Procedure

A. Fill the jar half full with water.

B. Cover the jar with plastic wrap. Hold the plastic wrap in place with a rubber band.

C. Place the jar in a sunny window. Leave it in the window for a few hours.
  1. What do you think will happen inside the jar?

D. Observe what has happened inside the jar.
  2. What do you see on the underside of the plastic wrap?
  3. Where did it come from?
  4. Why did you place the jar in a sunny window?

Conclusion

1. How is what happened inside the jar like the water cycle?
2. Where did evaporation take place?
3. Where did condensation take place?

Using science ideas

How could you speed up the cycle in the jar?

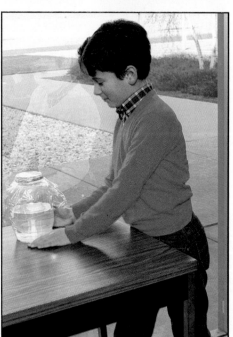

Ideas to Remember

▶ The earth is heated by energy from the sun.

▶ Seasons are caused by differences in how sunlight strikes the earth.

▶ Land and dark-colored surfaces absorb more sunlight than water and light-colored surfaces.

▶ Water from the earth's surface evaporates into the air.

▶ Clouds form when water vapor in the air changes to tiny droplets of water.

▶ Precipitation falls from clouds as snow, rain, or sleet.

▶ The water on the earth moves in a cycle.

Reviewing the Chapter

SCIENCE WORDS

A. Write the letter of the term that best matches the definition. Not all the terms will be used.

1. Moving air
2. Small ice crystals
3. Something that happens over and over again
4. A cloud near the ground
5. Frozen raindrops
6. A name for rain, snow, or sleet

    a. precipitation
    b. fog
    c. sleet
    d. dew
    e. frost
    f. wind
    g. cycle

B. Unscramble each group of letters to find a science term from the chapter. Then copy the sentences below. Use one term to complete each sentence.

1. dloucs
2. lasekowfns
3. trewa lycec
4. Water vapor that freezes into ice crystals forms ____.
5. The moving of water from the oceans to the air and back to the oceans is called a ____.
6. When water vapor in the air changes to tiny droplets of water, ____ form.

UNDERSTANDING IDEAS

A. The sentences describe the water cycle. Write the numbers of the sentences to show the correct order.

1. Energy from the sun changes water to water vapor.
2. Most of the water returns to the oceans.
3. Winds blow the clouds over land.
4. Water vapor rises and condenses to form clouds.
5. Clouds meet cool air, and rain or snow falls.

B. Choose one of the drawings to answer each question below.

1. Which drawing shows the season in which the part of the earth where you live is tilted toward the sun?

2. Which drawing shows the season in which sunlight strikes the earth at a slant?

USING IDEAS

Imagine that you are a weather reporter. Write a report about today's weather. Use science terms from this chapter in your report.

THINKING LIKE A SCIENTIST

You may be able to answer some of these questions just by thinking about them. To answer other questions, you may have to do some research.

1. Suppose two cities had the same temperature one day. They also had the same amount of water in the air. One city had clouds covering it at night and the other did not. Which city would have a cooler night? Explain your answer.

2. When a volcano erupts it shoots tons of ash into the sky. Sometimes, after a large volcano erupts, the earth is cooler for several months. What do you think happens at these times?

3. Astronauts sometimes have a problem with water in the air. They have a machine like a vacuum cleaner to help them take showers aboard the space shuttle. What do you think this machine does?

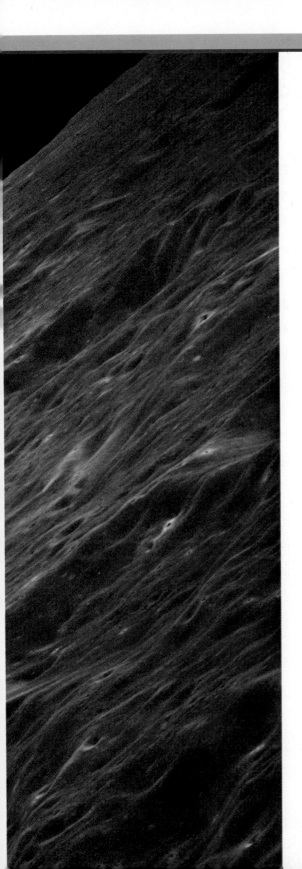

Chapter 12

Sun, Moon, and Planets

The earth has many neighbors out in space. The sun and the moon are important neighbors of the earth. The sun and the moon affect the earth in many ways.

This picture was taken from the moon. The body in space is the earth. You can see that only part of it is lighted by the sun. It is day on the lighted part. It is night on the dark part.

In this chapter you will learn about the sun and the moon. You will also learn about other bodies in space.

Looking at the Moon and the Sun

What is it like on the moon and the sun?

Look at the two balls in the first picture. You can see that they are not the same size. Look at the other picture. Each ball is in a different place. The two balls now appear to be the same size. Why is this?

The bodies in space appear smaller than they really are. Sometimes smaller bodies in space look bigger than larger ones.

At night, the moon appears larger than any of the stars in the sky. But the moon is really much smaller than any of the stars. The closer to the earth a body in space is, the larger it appears to be. The moon is the earth's closest neighbor in space.

Different-sized balls

The sun is much larger than the moon. But it is much farther from the earth than the moon is. Large bodies like the sun look smaller when they are far away.

The moon does not give off its own light. Instead it reflects light from the sun. The sun is the source of light for the earth and the moon.

In some ways the moon and the earth are alike. Both are covered by rocks and soil. Both have uneven surfaces. Mountains, valleys, and large flat areas are found on both the moon and the earth. But the earth's surface is always being changed by moving water and wind. The moon's surface does not change. Can you tell why?

Mountains on the moon

Mountains on the earth

Science & TECHNOLOGY

◄ Did you ever wonder what it would be like to travel on the surface of the moon? On some trips to the moon, astronauts used the Lunar Rover. The Rover had four wheels and seats for two people. It moved at a top speed of 16 kilometers an hour.

Do you think it would be a good idea to use the Rover on the surface of the earth?

When you look at the moon, the mountains are the light-colored areas. Can you find these areas in the picture below?

There are also dark areas on the moon. Find them in the picture. These areas are very smooth. Long ago people thought these areas were large bodies of water. So they called them seas. Today scientists know there is no water on the moon. The dark areas are large flat plains.

The surface of the moon is also marked with craters (krā′tərz). A **crater** is a hollow area that looks like the inside of a bowl. Most scientists think that many of the craters were formed when rocks from space crashed on the surface of the moon.

Areas of the moon

Can you make craters?

To do this, you will need some damp sand, several small rocks, a flat pan, and a ruler. Pour the sand into the pan. Make it about 4 centimeters deep. Use the ruler to smooth the surface of the sand. Hold a rock about 20 centimeters above the sand. Drop it into the sand. Do this with the other rocks. Make sure you drop the rocks in different places in the sand. Carefully pick each rock out of the sand. How does the surface of the sand compare with the surface of the moon?

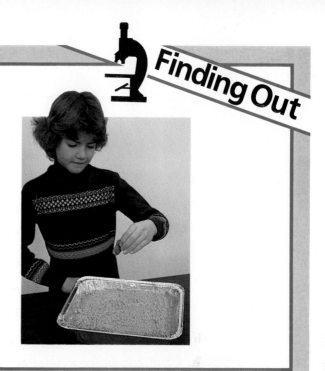

The sun is like the earth and the moon in shape. But the sun is a much larger ball. The surface of the sun is very different from the surfaces of the earth and the moon. The sun is made of hot, glowing gases. These hot gases are very active. Sometimes they seem to explode from the surface of the sun. In doing this, they form streams of gas that glow. These streams of gas are called **sun flares.** They shoot out far into space.

Sun

Look at the picture of the sun. Find the sun flare. You can also see light and dark areas on the surface of the sun. These areas show differences in temperature. The light areas are hotter than the dark areas.

Motions in Space

How do the earth and the moon move?

Do you know that you are moving even when you are standing still? You are moving because the earth is moving. The earth is always moving around the sun. A body in space that moves around a larger body is called a **satellite** (sat′ə līt). The earth is a satellite of the sun. The moon is also a satellite. It moves around the earth.

Satellites, like the earth and the moon, always travel in a path around a larger body. This path is called an **orbit** (ôr′bit). In the drawing you can see the earth's orbit around the sun. You can also see the moon's orbit around the earth. Which orbit is longer?

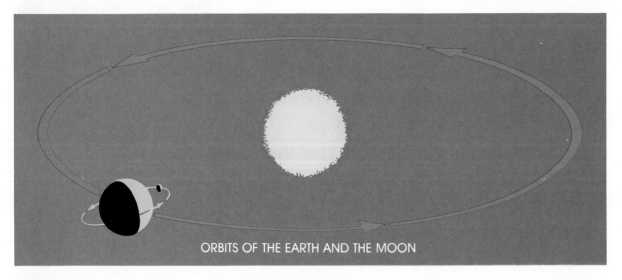

ORBITS OF THE EARTH AND THE MOON

The movement of the earth and the moon in their orbits is called a **revolution** (rev ə lü′shən). It takes the earth a year to make one revolution around the sun. It takes the moon about a month to make one revolution around the earth.

Most bodies in space also move in another way. They spin. Their spinning motion is like the spinning of a top. The picture of the globe shows how the earth spins. The flag will go around once before it returns to the same position. This full turn is called a **rotation** (rō tā′shən). The earth makes one full rotation every 24 hours. What period of time is 24 hours? Bodies in space rotate at different speeds. The moon rotates only once in about a month.

Spinning a top

Spinning a globe

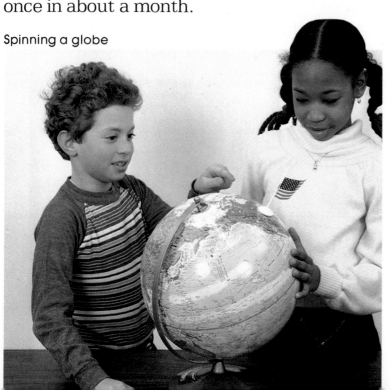

Phases of the Moon

Why does the moon always look different?

Different moon phases

You have probably noticed how the shape of the moon seems to change. On some nights, you may see only a small part of the moon. On other nights, the moon may look big and round. These changes in how the moon looks are called **phases** (fā′ziz).

The moon orbits around the earth about once a month. How much of the moon you can see depends on where the moon is in its orbit around the earth. During the first half of the moon's orbit, more and more of the moon can be seen each night. During the second half, less and less of the moon can be seen. The drawing shows the changes in the position of the moon. Each numbered step shows a different phase of the moon.

1. New moon—The dark side of the moon faces the earth. The moon is in the daytime sky. We cannot see the moon during the new moon phase.

2. First quarter moon—The moon is now one fourth of the way around its orbit of the earth. One half of the lighted side of the moon can be seen from the earth during the first-quarter moon phase.

3. Full moon—The moon is now halfway around its orbit. How much of the lighted half of the moon can you see? After this phase less and less of the moon can be seen each night.

4. Last quarter moon—The moon is now three fourths of the way around its orbit.

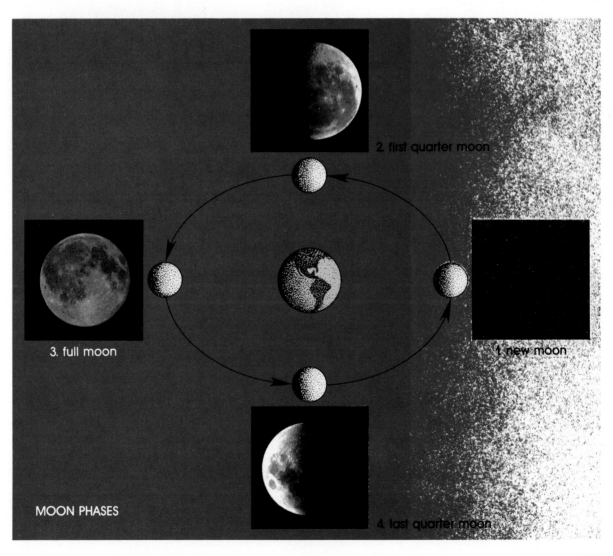

2. first quarter moon

3. full moon

1. new moon

MOON PHASES

4. last quarter moon

Eclipses

These children are playing a game. They are trying to see who can make the most unusual shadow. Objects that block the path of light make shadows.

Making shadows

The earth and the moon are large bodies that block the sun's light. In doing so, they make shadows. Sometimes the earth and the moon pass into each other's shadows. When one body passes into the shadow of another, an **eclipse** (i klips') occurs.

At full moon the earth is between the sun and the moon. As the moon orbits the earth, it sometimes enters the shadow the earth makes in space. The drawing shows how the earth's shadow falls on the moon. When this happens, the moon does not get light from the sun. The moon seems to disappear into the shadow. This is called an **eclipse of the moon.**

At new moon the moon is between the sun and the earth. Sometimes the moon blocks the sun's light from part of the earth. The drawing shows how the moon's shadow falls on the earth. This is an **eclipse of the sun.** You can see that the moon's shadow only falls on a small area of the earth. Where must you be to see an eclipse of the sun?

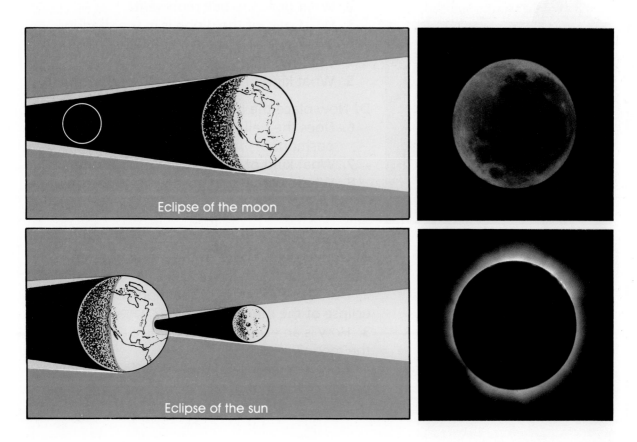

Eclipse of the moon

Eclipse of the sun

How do eclipses take place?

Materials globe / flashlight / small ball

Procedure
A. Work with a partner. Place a globe on a table. Stand one meter from the globe and hold a flashlight.

B. Darken the room and turn on the flashlight. The light should be shining on the globe.
   1. What does the flashlight represent?

C. Have your partner hold a small ball between the globe and the flashlight. You should be able to see a shadow on the globe.
   2. What does the ball represent?
   3. What part of the globe is in the shadow?
   4. What would you see if you were in the shadow?
   5. What kind of eclipse does this represent?

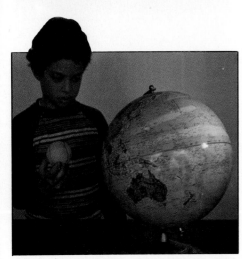

D. Now place the ball behind the globe.
   6. Does the ball receive any light in this position?
   7. What kind of eclipse does this represent?
   8. Where would you have to be to see this kind of eclipse?

Conclusion
1. During what phase of the moon does an eclipse of the sun take place?
2. During what phase of the moon does an eclipse of the moon take place?
3. How is an eclipse of the sun like an eclipse of the moon?
4. How is an eclipse of the sun different from an eclipse of the moon?

The Planets

What are planets?

The earth is not the only body that
revolves around the sun. Other large bodies
revolve around the sun. They are called
planets (plan'its). There are nine planets.
The earth, the other planets, and the sun are
all part of a large system. This system is
called the **solar system** (sō' lər   sis'təm).

You can see the sun and the planets in the
drawing. Each planet has its own orbit
around the sun. Which planet is nearest the

THE SOLAR SYSTEM

How are the planets different from each other?

Materials string / pencil / ruler / large file card / large sheet of white paper / scissors / books about planets / tape

Planet	Length of string in centimeters
Mercury	1
Venus	2
Earth	2½
Mars	1½
Jupiter	28
Saturn	23
Uranus	10
Neptune	11½
Pluto	1½

Procedure

A. Your teacher will help you and your classmates to form nine groups. There will be one group for each of the nine planets. Write the name of your planet on a large file card.

B. Draw a model of your planet. To do this, tie a piece of string to a pencil. You will use the string and the pencil to draw a circle.

C. Look at the chart to find out how much string you need to draw your planet. Measure the distance from the pencil to the correct place on the string. Mark the string.

D. Hold the marked part of the string and use the pencil to draw a circle on a piece of paper as shown.

E. Look in a book about planets. Find out what your planet looks like. Then mark and color your planet. Cut the planet out.

F. Tape your planet and the card with its name to a wall. Place it with the other planets in its correct order from the sun.

G. Look in books about planets. Find out as much as you can about your planet. Write a report.

Conclusion

How are the planets different from each other?

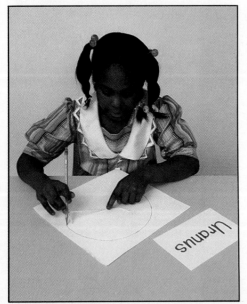

sun? Which planet is farthest away from the sun? Mercury (mėr′kyər ē) and Venus (vē′nəs) are closer to the sun than the earth is. These planets are also hotter than the earth. Mars (märz), Jupiter (jü′pə tər), Saturn (sat′ərn), Uranus (yùr′ə nəs), Neptune (nep′tün), and Pluto (plü′tō) are farther from the sun than the earth. The farther a planet is from the sun, the colder it is on that planet. Which planet is the coldest?

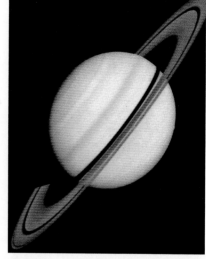

Saturn

Ideas to Remember

► The surfaces of the earth, the moon, and the sun are different from each other.

► The earth and the moon revolve and rotate.

► Changes in how the moon looks from the earth are called phases.

► An eclipse takes place when the earth or the moon passes into the other's shadow.

► The sun and the planets make up the solar system.

Reviewing the Chapter

SCIENCE WORDS

A. Copy the sentences below. Use science terms from the chapter to complete the sentences.

   1. A body in space that moves around a larger body is called a _____.

   2. The path on which the earth travels around the sun is an _____.

   3. The movement of the moon around the earth is a _____.

   4. The spinning motion of the earth is called a _____.

   5. When the earth or the moon passes into the other's shadow, an _____ occurs.

   6. The sun and the planets make up the _____.

B. Write the letter of the term that best matches the definition. Not all the terms will be used.

   1. Hollow areas on the moon's surface
   2. Streams of gas from the sun's surface
   3. Changes in how the moon looks
   4. Bodies that orbit the sun
   5. Path of a satellite

   a. phases
   b. orbit
   c. sun flares
   d. craters
   e. eclipse
   f. planets

UNDERSTANDING IDEAS

A. Write *T* for the sentences that are true. Rewrite false sentences to make them true.

   1. The earth is a satellite of the moon.
   2. The dark areas on the moon are plains.
   3. The earth and the moon revolve and rotate.
   4. The earth makes one revolution every 24 hours.

   5. The moon is smaller than any of the stars.
   6. The moon reflects the light of the sun.

B. Explain the difference between an eclipse of the sun and an eclipse of the moon. Make a drawing to show each kind of eclipse.

USING IDEAS

You can measure and map the locations of the planets. To do this, you will need a metric ruler, a meterstick, and some paper tape. Use a piece of tape that is at least 4 meters long. Label one end of the tape *Sun*. Then look at the table below. The table shows how far each planet is from the sun. Measure and mark the location of each planet.

Planet	Distance in centimeters
Mercury	4
Venus	7
Earth	10
Mars	15
Jupiter	52
Saturn	95
Uranus	192
Neptune	300
Pluto	395

THINKING LIKE A SCIENTIST

You may be able to answer some of these questions just by thinking about them. To answer other questions, you may have to do some research.

1. Sometimes scientists can figure out answers to questions without observing. Scientists are pretty sure how craters on the moon were formed. They have never watched one form. But they have seen many craterlike shapes formed on the earth. How could you demonstrate how a crater forms?

2. The earth revolves and rotates. Many things around you revolve and rotate. Name three objects that revolve and three that rotate.

3. Do you think there could be more than nine planets in our solar system? If so, why have we not yet discovered them?

Science in Careers

Everyone needs and uses materials from the earth.

Farmers and **ranchers** use the soil to grow food.

Soil scientists study soil to find ways to make it better.

Geologists (jē ol' ə jists) study the earth's crust. They look for oil, minerals, and other natural resources.

Soil scientist

Seismologist

Chemists find ways to use materials from the crust.

Seismologists (sīz mol' ə jists) study earthquakes. They try to find out what the inside of the earth is like.

Astronomers (ə stron' əm ə rz) and **astronauts** (as'trə nôts) are space scientists. They explore space, using telescopes or spacecraft. They study the sun, moon, and stars.

Astronaut

242

People in Science

HUGO BENIOFF
(1899–   )

Hugo Benioff is a scientist who studied the shock waves produced by earthquakes. He designed and built instruments to measure the shock waves. The instruments are called seismographs (sīz′mə grafs). Earthquakes occur along lines called faults. Benioff showed how shock waves produced after an earthquake are related to the size of the fault.

The San Andreas Fault in California

Developing Skills

WORD SKILLS

A compound word is made up of two or more words. Each word has a different meaning. When the words are put together, the new compound word has another meaning. For example, the words *water* and *fall* together make the compound word *waterfall*.

Make compound words by matching words from group **A** with words from group **B**.

A	
earth	sun
air	work
water	light
moon	flood
chalk	wind

B	
plane	house
proof	beam
fall	quake
flow	board
light	bench

READING A BAR GRAPH

A bar graph can be used to compare information. The bar graph on the next page shows how much coal we get from different states. Use the bar graph to answer these questions.

1. From which state do we get the most coal?

2. From which state do we get the least coal?

3. From which state do we get more coal, West Virginia or Illinois?

4. From which state do we get more coal, Pennsylvania or Wyoming?

5. From which state do we get more coal, Virginia or Texas?

6. From which state do we get the least amount of coal, Virginia, Montana, or Indiana?

7. Which amount is larger, the amount of coal we get from Ohio, Texas, and West Virginia or the amount of coal we get from Kentucky?

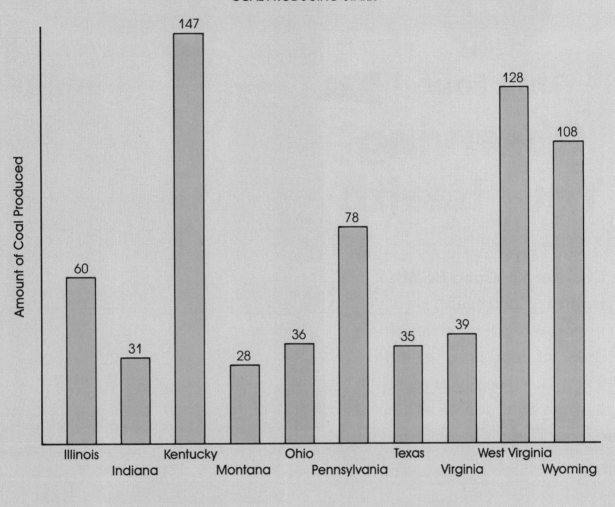

COAL-PRODUCING STATES

USING THINKING SKILLS

Coal is an important resource. Coal takes millions of years to form. There is a limited amount of coal in the earth. Think about this as you answer the following questions.

1. Use a reference book to find out the different ways coal is taken from the earth. Which way do you think is the best way to take coal from the earth? Explain your answer.

2. Since it takes so long for coal to form, should we take only a little coal from the earth at a time? Explain your answer.

Unit Four

Observing Your Health

Chapter 13—Good Health Habits   Good health is very important. But good health does not happen by itself. There are things you must learn to do to stay healthy.

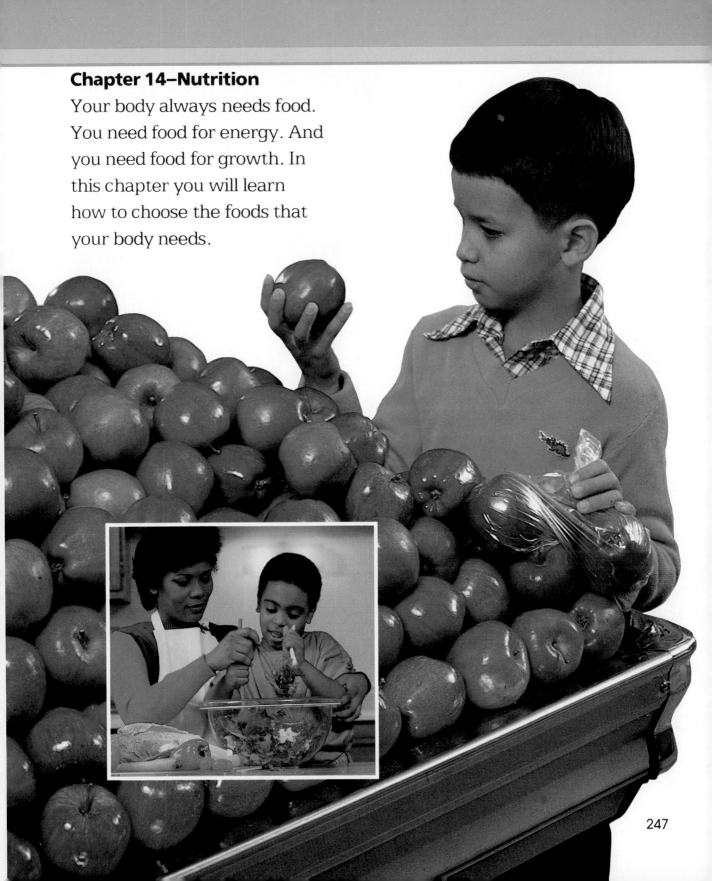

Chapter 14—Nutrition

Your body always needs food.
You need food for energy. And
you need food for growth. In
this chapter you will learn
how to choose the foods that
your body needs.

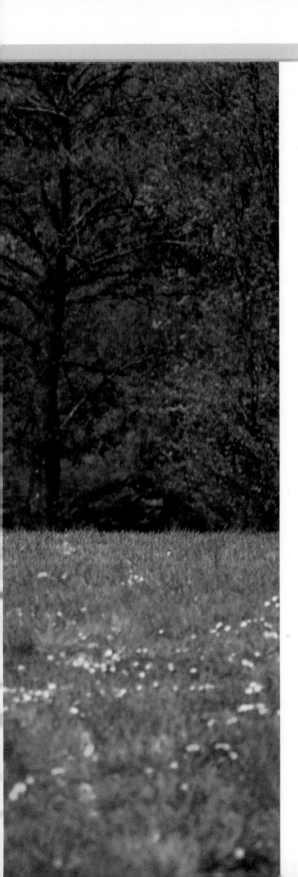

Chapter 13

Good Health Habits

You can do many things to keep your body healthy. When your body is healthy, it works the way it should. You feel good. Knowing what to do to keep your body healthy can keep you from becoming sick. The things you learn now about having a healthy body will be important all your life.

In this chapter you will learn about keeping your body clean. You will learn why exercise and rest are important. You will also learn about safety while riding a bicycle. The things you learn in this chapter should become part of your good health habits.

Keeping Yourself Clean

What are some ways of keeping your body clean?

Do you do certain things each day without thinking about them? Things that we do without having to think about them are called **habits** (hab'its). People have good habits and bad habits. To be healthy, you should practice good health habits.

One good health habit is to keep yourself clean. Being clean helps keep germs (jėrmz) away. **Germs** are harmful living things that can make people sick. They are too small to see.

One way to be clean is to wash your hands with soap and water before you eat. Washing with soap and water helps to keep

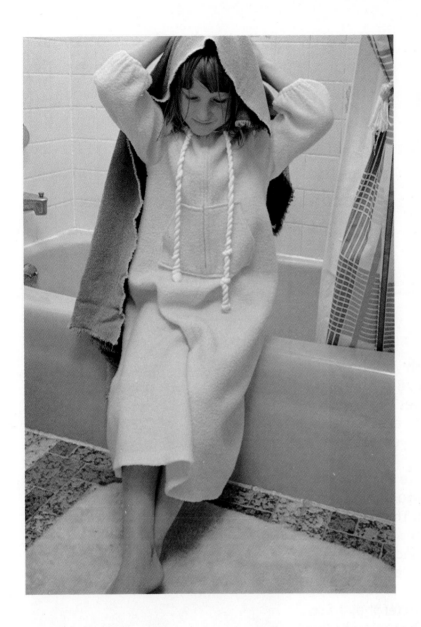

germs from getting in your food. Do you always wash your hands before you eat?

Taking a bath or shower is another way to be clean. Do you take a bath or shower every day? After a bath or shower you will feel and smell clean.

Another way to be clean is to wash your hair. Some people wash their hair every day. Others wash their hair only once a week. You should wash your hair with shampoo.

After you wash your hair, you should dry it and brush it. Brushing your hair makes it soft and shiny. Brushing your hair between washings also helps to keep it healthy.

You know that you wash your body and hair to remove germs. But how are germs kept out of your eyes? You wash around the outside of your eyes with soap and water. But your eyes wash themselves with tears.

Glands near your eyes are always making tears. Each time you blink, tears are spread over your eyes. They keep your eyes from drying. They also keep your eyes clear. When a speck of dirt gets into your eye, it is usually washed out by tears.

What happens to tears after they have done their job? They go through a hole in the inner corner of each eye. If you look closely, you will see it. Small tubes then carry the tears into your nose. You do not notice this until you start to cry. Then the tears make your nose run.

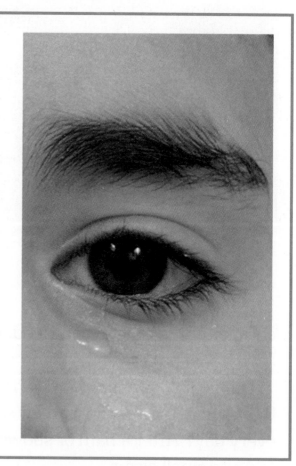

How does soap change oil?

Materials   small jar or other container / dropper / cooking oil / liquid soap / spoon / cold water / warm water

Procedure
A. Fill a jar almost to the top with cold water. Using a dropper, add three drops of oil. Move the jar gently in a small circle.
   1. How does the oil look?
   2. What happens to the oil?

B. Add three drops of liquid soap to the water and oil. Stir with a spoon.
   3. What happens to the oil?

C. Empty the jar. Then fill it almost to the top with warm water. Add three drops of oil to the warm water.
   4. Does the oil look different in warm water than it did in cold water?

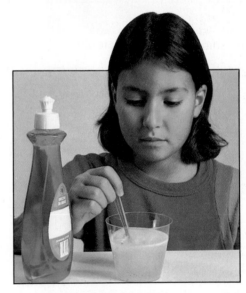

D. Add three drops of liquid soap to the warm water and oil. Stir with a spoon.
   5. What happens to the oil?

Conclusion
How does soap change oil?

Using science ideas
1. Shampoo is a soap used for washing hair. What happens to oil in water when shampoo is added to the water?
2. Why should you use shampoo when you wash your hair?

Teeth Care

Your teeth are very important to you. Learning to take care of your teeth now will help prevent problems when you are older. It is best to brush your teeth after every meal and before bedtime.

It is important to brush your teeth properly. You should always use a good toothbrush. Many dentists say you should brush your teeth with short back-and-forth strokes. The brush should be held gently against the teeth. The pictures show where to place a toothbrush when brushing the different surfaces of your teeth.

Brushing your teeth helps to remove bits of food from spaces between the teeth. It

Brushing outside back teeth

Brushing inside back teeth

Brushing inside front teeth

Brushing outside front teeth

also removes plaque (plak) from teeth. **Plaque** is a sticky film made up of tiny germs. It causes teeth to decay. A tooth decays when the tiny germs in plaque change certain foods into a harmful substance. The harmful substance can make a hole in the outside covering of a tooth. A hole in a tooth is called a **cavity** (kav'ə tē). If a cavity is not repaired by a dentist, it may become larger.

Cavities in teeth

Flossing teeth

Brushing often does not remove all the food and plaque from your teeth. A special kind of thread called **dental floss** (flôs) must be used. The picture shows how teeth are flossed. You should floss your teeth once a day.

255

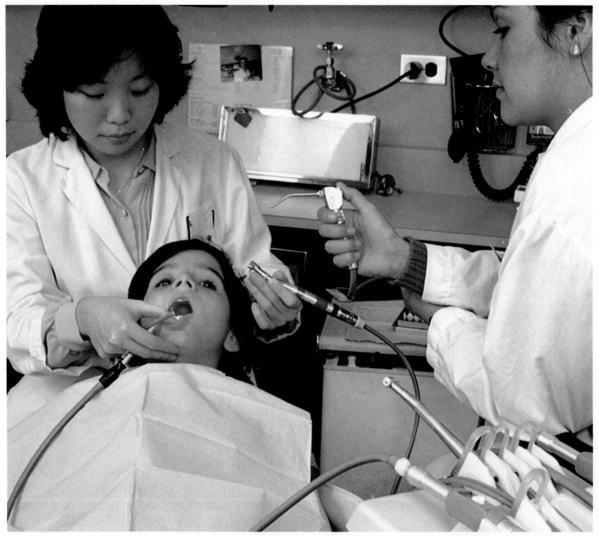
Dentist cleaning teeth

A dentist can help you keep your teeth healthy. By having a checkup you can make sure little problems do not become big problems. The dentist can clean your teeth and repair cavities. When you visit your dentist ask about the best way to take care of your teeth.

Exercise and Sleep

Why are exercise and rest important to your health?

Regular exercise is important to your health. Exercise makes your body work hard. Exercise keeps the muscles (mus′əls) in your body strong. Muscles that are well exercised can work longer without getting tired. Exercise also makes your heart stronger.

You can get exercise in many different ways. You can walk or ride a bicycle. You can jump rope or swim. You can play games such as softball.

An exercise class

Jumping rope

You should exercise every day for at least 15 minutes. Exercise will then become a good health habit. You should begin exercising slowly. This way you will not hurt your muscles.

You can exercise by yourself. Some exercises you can do by yourself are walking, running, or jumping rope. You can also exercise by playing games with your friends. You can play soccer or volleyball. You can run races with your friends.

Your body needs rest as well as exercise. Sometimes you rest by sitting still. When you are very tired, you usually sleep. You may even take a nap during the day if you are tired.

Your body needs some sleep every day. When you sleep, your body does not work hard. Your breathing slows down and your heart beats more slowly. Sleep gives your body a chance to repair itself. It also allows your mind to rest. Without sleep, your body becomes tired and worn-out. Then you might get sick.

People need different amounts of sleep. Some people need more sleep than others. Small babies sleep about 20 hours a day. You probably sleep 8 to 10 hours a day. Older people need only about 6 hours of sleep a day. You know you have had enough sleep if you wake up feeling rested. How many hours of sleep do you get each day?

What are some stretching exercises?

Procedure

A. Do this exercise. Stand up straight with your arms at your side. Spread your feet a little. Move your head in a circle from right to left three times. Try to make your chin touch your chest. Now move your head in a circle from left to right three times.

 1. What muscles are you stretching?

B. Do another exercise. Stand up straight with your feet apart. Raise both arms over your head. Stand on your toes and reach as high as you can. Hold this position while you count to five. Do this three times.

 2. What muscles are you stretching?

C. Do the exercise shown in the pictures. Stand up straight with your feet apart. Hold your arms straight out at your side. Keep your arms and legs straight as you bend to touch your toes. Touch the toes on your left foot with your right hand. Then come back to your starting position. Now touch the toes on your right foot with your left hand. Do this exercise three times.

 3. What muscles are you stretching?

Conclusion

1. How do stretching exercises help your muscles?
2. How do your muscles feel after stretching?

Safety Habits

How do safety habits help you
to stay healthy?

Safety is an important part of staying
healthy. Good safety habits help prevent
accidents that might hurt you.

You should be very careful when you ride
a bicycle. You are riding safely if you do
these things.

- Watch out for cars and people.
- Watch for rocks and holes in the street.
- Obey all traffic signals.
- Follow the same traffic rules that people
  driving cars do.
- Ride in the same direction in which
  traffic is moving.
- Ride next to the curb.
- Ride on bicycle paths whenever possible.

Riding safely

Stopping at an intersection

Many bicycle accidents can be prevented. Most can be prevented if you make sure that drivers of cars can see you. Always wear light-colored clothing when you ride. A flag on your bicycle also makes you easier to see in the daytime. In dim light, reflectors on your bicycle will help drivers to see you. Your bicycle should have reflectors on the front and back wheels. You should also have reflectors on the pedals. When you ride with a friend, always ride in single file. Be sure to use hand signals before you stop or make a turn. If you follow these rules, bicycle riding will be fun and safe.

Finding Out

Do you practice good health habits?

At the end of the day, answer these questions about yourself. Do this for a week. Keep a record of your answers in a notebook. At the end of the week, look at all your answers. What can you do to improve your health habits?

1. I exercised today.	Yes	No
2. I brushed my teeth after every meal.	Yes	No
3. I rested today.	Yes	No
4. I took a bath or shower today.	Yes	No
5. I used hand signals when I rode my bicycle today.	Yes	No
6. I washed my hands before meals today.	Yes	No

Bicycle inspection

Ideas to Remember

▶ Good health habits help you to stay healthy.

▶ Keeping yourself clean helps keep germs away.

▶ Taking care of your teeth can prevent cavities.

▶ Exercise keeps muscles in your body strong.

▶ Getting enough rest is important for good health.

▶ Practicing good safety habits will help keep you healthy.

Reviewing the Chapter

A. Use all the terms below to complete the sentences.

germs   plaque   cavity   dental floss

   Learning to care for your teeth is important. Brushing helps to remove bits of food and __1__ from teeth. A special kind of thread called __2__ can also be used to clean teeth. A tooth decays when tiny __3__ in plaque change certain foods into a harmful substance. The harmful substance will make a hole in the outside covering of the tooth. This hole is called a __4__.

B. Unscramble each group of letters to find a science term from the chapter. Write a sentence using each term.

1. batihs   **2.** stinted
3. serexiec   **4.** ayseft

A. A *cause* makes things happen. An *effect* is what happens. For each pair of sentences, write which is the cause and which is the effect.

1. a. You do not get enough sleep.
   b. Your body is tired and worn out.
2. a. You exercise every day.
   b. The muscles in your body can work longer.
3. a. You have few cavities.
   b. You brush your teeth properly.
4. a. You wash your hair with shampoo.
   b. Your hair is always soft and shiny.

B. Explain why exercise and rest are important to your health.

C. List three health habits you should practice in taking care of your teeth.

USING IDEAS

1. Use two or three sheets of drawing paper to make a booklet. On each page, draw a picture of yourself practicing a good health habit. Draw a picture on the cover. Think of a title for your booklet.

2. Make a health or safety poster. Choose one or more good health or safety habits for your poster. Think of a title for your poster.

THINKING LIKE A SCIENTIST

You may be able to answer some of these questions just by thinking about them. To answer other questions, you may have to do some research.

1. How do you think your eyelashes help to protect your eyes?

2. Inventors often help to solve science problems. Name five inventions that make it easier for people to practice good health habits at home.

3. Pretend you are doing a study on tooth decay. The people in Group A eat mostly fresh fruits, vegetables, and meats. Those in Group B eat large amounts of candy, cake, and soft drinks. After a year, the people in Group B have many more cavities than those in Group A. What conclusions could you draw from these results?

4. Why is riding a bicycle right after a storm a dangerous thing to do?

Chapter 14

Nutrition

Did you ever hear someone say, "You are what you eat"? The food that you eat really becomes part of you. This is why eating good food is important. Some foods give your body the energy it needs. Other foods are important for keeping muscles and bones strong. Some foods help your body to grow and to repair itself. How do you know which foods to eat? Which foods are healthful and which are not?

In this chapter you will learn why food is so important for your body. You will learn about the different kinds of foods you eat. You will also learn how to have good eating habits.

The Need for Food

Why do you need to eat food?

The food you eat is important to your body in many ways. Food provides the energy you need for everything you do. You are using energy while you are reading this book. You use a lot more energy when you jump rope or run. You even use energy when you sleep. This energy comes from food.

There is energy in all foods. But some foods have more energy than others.

Using less energy

Using more energy

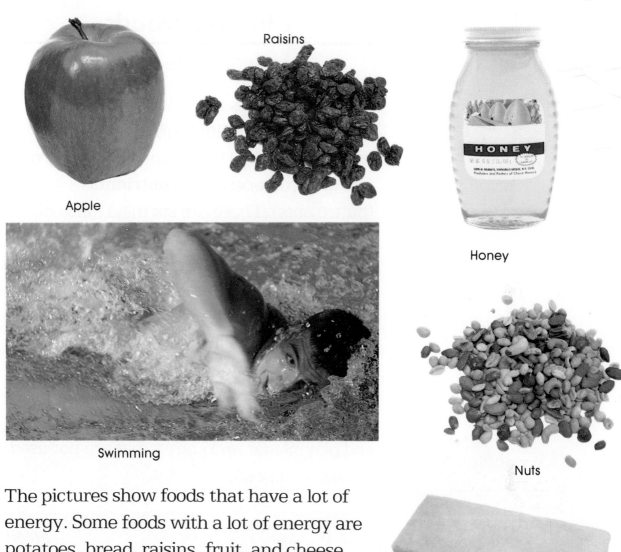

Raisins

Apple

Honey

Swimming

Nuts

The pictures show foods that have a lot of energy. Some foods with a lot of energy are potatoes, bread, raisins, fruit, and cheese. You should eat foods like these when you are very active. When you are not very active, you are not using as much energy. You should eat foods that do not have as much energy. Vegetables such as lettuce and tomatoes have less energy than the foods in the pictures.

Cheese

Kinds of Foods

How are nutrients used by your body?

Your body uses many kinds of foods. The food you eat contains many things. The parts of the foods that help your body grow and give you energy are **nutrients** (nü′trē ənts). There are six main kinds of nutrients. They are (1) sugar and starch, (2) fat, (3) protein (prō′tēn), (4) vitamins (vī′tə mins), (5) minerals, and (6) water.

Sugar and **starch** give your body quick energy. Apples, bananas, oranges, honey, and other sweet foods contain sugar. Bread, potatoes, and noodles have starch. All these foods give you the energy you need to work and play. Sugar and starch that are not used for energy are stored as fat.

Using quick energy

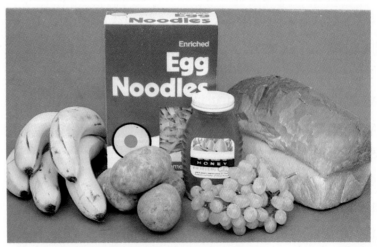
Some quick-energy foods

Fat also has a lot of energy. Fat has more than twice as much energy as sugar or starch. Your body stores the fat that it does not use. This stored fat can be used when your body needs extra energy. Stored fat also helps to keep your body warm. Having too much fat stored in your body is not healthy. Butter, cheese, nuts, and milk have fat. All the foods in the picture have fat.

Measuring growth

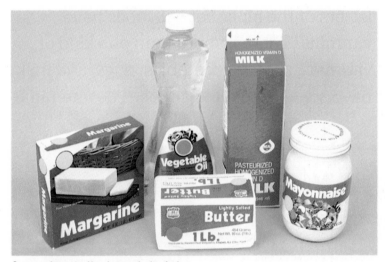

Some foods that contain fat

Protein is needed for your muscles, bones, and other body parts to grow. While you are young and growing, you need lots of protein. The boy in the picture needs the foods shown to grow. Since you cannot store protein, you should eat foods that have protein every day. Meat, eggs, beans, and cheese are foods that have protein.

Some protein foods

Minerals also are needed for growth. They help your body rebuild worn-out parts as well. Certain minerals help build strong bones and teeth. They are found in milk, cheese, and vegetables. Iron is an important mineral. It is important for healthy blood. Iron is found in liver and green vegetables.

Vitamins help your body to work the way it should. You need many different kinds of vitamins. Most vitamins are named after letters of the alphabet. All foods have vitamins. There is more than one kind of vitamin B. Leafy vegetables, eggs, and milk have some of the B vitamins. The vitamin B group is important for growth and energy. Oranges and other fruits have vitamin C that helps to keep you healthy. Vitamin D in milk helps your teeth and bones stay strong.

Water is a very important nutrient. You should drink six to eight glasses of water every day. Some of the water you need is found in milk or fruit juice. There is also a lot

of water in some fruits and vegetables. You cannot live without water. Over half your body is made of water.

It is important that you have all six kinds of nutrients each day. But how can you tell if the foods you eat have all the nutrients you need? One way to find out is to read the labels on boxes, cans, or jars of foods. The labels list the nutrients in the foods.

NUTRITION INFORMATION

SERVING SIZE: 1 OZ. (28.4 g. ABOUT ½ CUP) CEREAL ALONE OR WITH ½ CUP VITAMIN D FORTIFIED WHOLE MILK.
SERVINGS PER PACKAGE: 12

FLAKES OF WHOLE CORN

	CEREAL	WITH MILK
CALORIES	110	180
PROTEIN	2 g	6 g
CARBOHYDRATE	24 g	30 g
FAT	1 g	5 g
SODIUM	185 mg	245 mg

PERCENTAGE OF U.S. RECOMMENDED DAILY ALLOWANCES (U.S. RDA)

FLAKES OF WHOLE CORN

	CEREAL	WITH MILK
PROTEIN	4	10
VITAMIN A	25	30
VITAMIN C	25	25
THIAMIN	25	30
RIBOFLAVIN	25	35
NIACIN	25	25
CALCIUM	*	15
IRON	4	6
VITAMIN D	10	25
VITAMIN E	25	25
VITAMIN B₆	25	30
FOLIC ACID	25	25
VITAMIN B₁₂	25	30
PHOSPHORUS	6	20
MAGNESIUM	6	10
ZINC	25	30
COPPER	4	4

*CONTAINS LESS THAN 2% OF THE U.S. RDA OF THIS NUTRIENT.

INGREDIENTS LISTED IN ORDER OF PREDOMINANCE.
INGREDIENTS: WHOLE CORN KERNELS, MALT FLAVORING, SALT, BAKING SODA.

FORTIFIED WITH: VITAMIN C (SODIUM ASCORBATE AND ASCORBIC ACID), VITAMIN E (VITAMIN E ACETATE), NIACIN (NIACINAMIDE), ZINC (ZINC OXIDE), VITAMIN A (VITAMIN A PALMITATE), VITAMIN B₆ (PYRIDOXINE HYDROCHLORIDE), VITAMIN B₂ (RIBOFLAVIN), VITAMIN B₁ (THIAMIN HYDROCHLORIDE), FOLIC ACID, VITAMIN B₁₂ AND VITAMIN D₂.

Food label

Activity

What nutrients are in food?

Materials   food labels from 4 or more different foods

Procedure

A. Look at the food label in the picture on page 273.
1. Does the food contain protein?
2. Does the food contain carbohydrates (sugar or starch)?
3. What other nutrients does the food contain?

B. Make a chart like the one shown. The first line has been filled in as an example. The information is from the food label on page 273.

Food	Protein	Fat	Carbohydrates (sugar and starch)	Vitamins	Minerals
Cereal	✓	✓	✓	✓	✓

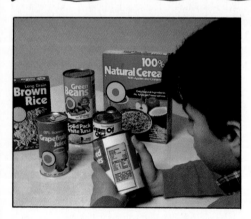

C. Look at food labels from four or more different foods. Fill in your chart with the information from the labels.
4. Which food has the most nutrients?
5. Which food has the fewest nutrients?

Conclusion
1. What nutrients are in foods? How do you know?
2. What other information about a food can you find out by reading the food label?

Food Groups

What are the four main food groups?

Your **diet** (dī′ət) is all the food you eat. You know that food has nutrients. If you are getting all the nutrients your body needs, you are eating a balanced diet. A balanced diet includes foods from each of the four food groups. The four food groups are (1) meats, (2) breads and cereals, (3) fruits and vegetables, and (4) milk products.

The meat group is made up of foods that have a lot of protein. Chicken, fish, meat, eggs, nuts, and dried beans are in this group.

Foods from the four food groups

You should eat at least two servings from the meat group every day.

The bread and cereal group is made up of foods that have a lot of starch. Rice, noodles, cereal, and bread are in this group. You should eat four or more servings from the bread and cereal group every day.

The fruit and vegetable group is made up of foods that have sugar, starch, minerals, and vitamins. The group includes all fruits and vegetables. You should eat at least four servings from this group every day.

The milk group is made up of foods that have vitamins, minerals, protein, and some fat. All the foods in this group come from milk. They include cheese, butter, and ice

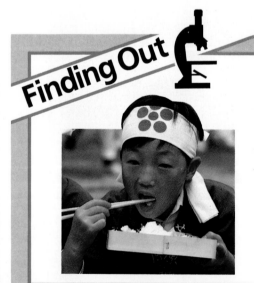

Finding Out

What is the diet of other people like?

People in other parts of the world eat foods that are different from the foods you eat. Children in Japan might eat rice with vegetables and fish for lunch. Children in Jamaica (je mā′kə) might eat black beans with pork and coconut for lunch.

Look in cookbooks and other books to find out what foods people in other countries eat. Do they eat foods from the four food groups?

cream. You should eat three servings from this group every day.

You should eat some foods from each group at every meal. The pictures show a balanced breakfast, lunch, and dinner. Can you tell which group each food comes from? If you eat food from each group every day, you will have a balanced diet.

Breakfast

Dinner

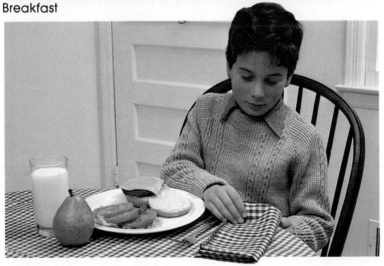

Lunch

What foods are in a balanced diet?

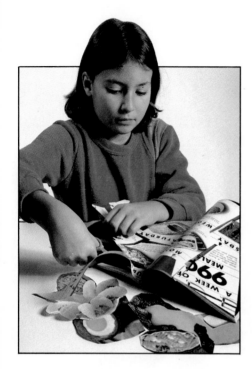

Materials   old magazines and newspapers / scissors / 3 large pieces of paper / paste / crayons

Procedure

A. Look through magazines and newspapers for pictures of food. Cut out the pictures.

B. Choose foods from the pictures to make a balanced breakfast. Paste the pictures on a piece of paper. If you cannot find pictures for certain foods, use crayons to draw them.

   1. What food groups are in your breakfast?
   2. What food groups are missing?

C. Repeat step **B,** but this time choose pictures to make a balanced lunch.

   3. What food groups are in your lunch?
   4. What food groups are missing?

D. Repeat step **B** again, this time choosing pictures to make a balanced dinner.

   5. What food groups are in your dinner?
   6. What food groups are missing?

Conclusion

1. How many servings from each food group are in the meals you planned?
2. What is a balanced diet?
3. What foods are in a balanced diet?

Using science ideas

Plan a balanced meal for a very active person. Plan another balanced meal for a person who is not active. How are the meals different?

Healthy Eating Habits

What are three healthy eating habits?

You know that you should eat three balanced meals a day. If you get hungry between meals, you should choose a snack from one of the four food groups. Snacks that are not good for you are foods with a lot of sugar and fat. They do not give you vitamins and minerals. Potato chips, cake, candy, and soft drinks are not good snack foods. What are some good snack foods?

The pictures show some snacks that are good for you. What food groups do these foods come from? Snacks that are good for you are part of a balanced diet. Eating a balanced diet is a healthy eating habit.

Cereal with milk

Peanut butter and celery

Cheese and crackers

Fresh foods

Another healthy eating habit is to eat fresh foods. Fresh foods are sometimes called natural foods. Fresh foods often have more vitamins and minerals than foods in cans, jars, or boxes.

You should eat only as much food as your body needs. If you eat more food than your body needs, the unused food will be stored as fat. By eating too much food, you may gain too much weight. If you do not eat enough food, your body cannot get the energy it needs. You may feel tired. You may lose weight. A doctor can tell you if you should gain or lose weight. A general rule is to eat only at mealtimes and only until you are full. And be sure to eat a balanced diet.

Look at the picture. You can see people playing basketball. What should be the eating habits of these people?

Ideas to Remember

▶ Food is the source of energy for everything you do.

▶ The six kinds of nutrients are sugar and starch, fat, protein, vitamins, minerals, and water.

▶ A balanced diet includes food from each of the four food groups.

▶ Vitamins help to keep your body working the way it should.

▶ Healthy eating habits are important for good health.

Reviewing the Chapter

A. Copy the sentences below. Use science terms from the chapter to complete the sentences.

1. The foods you eat are all part of your _____.
2. The parts of food that help your body grow and give you energy are called _____.
3. Two foods your body uses for quick energy are _____.
4. Foods stored in your body that can be used for extra energy are called _____.

B. Write the letter of the term that best matches the definition. Not all the terms will be used.

1. Food that contains starch
2. Nutrient that makes up over one half of your body
3. Food that contains sugar
4. Nutrients that help your body rebuild worn-out parts
5. Nutrients that are used for energy
6. Food that has fat in it

   a. apple
   b. vitamins
   c. nuts
   d. diet
   e. water
   f. bread
   g. minerals

UNDERSTANDING IDEAS

A. Identify each of the following.

1. I am a nutrient. I help your body to grow. I am found in meat, chicken, fish, eggs, and cheese. What am I?

2. I am a mineral. I am important for healthy blood. I am found in liver and green vegetables. What am I?

B. Name the six main kinds of nutrients.

C. Make a chart like the one shown. Write the names of some foods under the correct heading of the chart.

Meat group	Bread and cereal group	Fruit and vegetable group	Milk group

After completing the chart, tell which foods come from plants and which foods come from animals.

USING IDEAS

Plan a menu for breakfast, lunch, and dinner. Include the right amount of food from each of the four food groups.

THINKING LIKE A SCIENTIST

You may be able to answer some of these questions just by thinking about them. To answer other questions, you may have to do some research.

1. Long ago, sailors had a skin disease called scurvy (skĕr'vē). While sailing they did not eat oranges and other fresh fruits and vegetables. Fruits and vegetables did not stay fresh on the ship. While on shore the sailors ate fruits and vegetables. Then they did not get scurvy as often. Describe what you think was happening to the sailors' bodies.

2. Astronauts must have a balanced diet. Scientists did tests to learn which foods were easy to bring aboard a spacecraft. Which foods do you think are most difficult to cook, eat, and store in space?

Science in Careers

Many people help to keep you healthy. You can name **doctors, dentists,** and **nurses.** But there are many other health workers.

Many people work for city health departments. Among other duties they make sure that health laws are obeyed.

Food inspectors check meat, fruits, and vegetables before they are sold. They make sure the food did not come from diseased animals or plants.

Food inspectors

Nurse

Paramedics (par'ə med iks) work closely with doctors. They give emergency treatment to sick and injured people.

Pharmacists (fär'mə sists) make up the medicines ordered by doctors for sick people.

Dietitians (dī ə tish'ə nz) plan meals needed for good health.

Paramedics

People in Science

DR. JANE C. WRIGHT
(1919–)

Dr. Wright did not plan to be a doctor. Her goal was to become a famous artist. Today Dr. Wright teaches at the medical school where she was once a student. But her main interest is cancer research. She is trying to find a cure for cancer. She feels that someday cancer will be curable with drugs. Dr. Wright is trying to find those drugs.

Doctor doing cancer research

Developing Skills

Prefixes and suffixes are word parts. A prefix is added to the beginning of a base word. A suffix is added to the end of a base word. The tables show how some prefixes and suffixes change the meanings of words.

Use the tables to write meanings for these words.

1. cooler
2. seedless
3. dusty
4. reheat
5. mistrust
6. meatless
7. rewrap
8. unsafe

Prefix	Meaning	Example
mis-	wrong	misplace
re-	again	reopen
un-	not	unhappy

Suffix	Meaning	Example
-er	more	warmer
-less	without	waterless
-y	like	milky

You can learn many things by reading some tables. The table on the next page shows different nutrients. It tells where the nutrients are found. It also tells what the nutrients do. Use the table to answer the following questions.

1. In what foods can fats be found?

2. What nutrients are found in leafy vegetables?

3. In what foods can sugar and starch be found?

4. What does protein do for the body?

5. In what foods can vitamin D be found?

6. What does vitamin A do for the body?

7. What does iron do for the body?

8. What nutrients do eggs contain?

9. Which of the foods listed supply energy?

NUTRIENTS

Nutrients	What They Do	Where They Are Found
Fat	Supplies energy	Butter, nuts
Iron	Needed for healthy blood	Liver, meat, eggs
Protein	Needed for growth	Fish, meat, eggs, milk
Sugar and starch	Supply energy	Sugar, bread
Vitamin A	Needed for good eyesight and growth	Leafy vegetables, fruit, yellow vegetables
Vitamin C	Heals cuts	Oranges, tomatoes, potatoes
Vitamin D	Builds strong bones and teeth	Liver, eggs

USING THINKING SKILLS

An important part of being healthy is eating the right foods. It is important that you have all six kinds of nutrients every day.

1. Choose a country. Use books to find out what types of foods people in the country eat.

2. Most people in the world do not get enough nutrients. What can be done to help people around the world get enough food and nutrients? What can you and your classmates do to help?

Study Guide

Reading your book will help you learn more about the world around you. Your book will provide answers to many questions you may have about living things, the earth, space, matter, and energy.

On the following pages you will find questions from each lesson in your book. These questions will help test your understanding of the terms and ideas you read about. You will also find information about metric measurement.

There are three sections for each chapter. You can answer questions in the first section, "Lesson Questions," by using the information you read in each chapter. Careful reading will help answer these questions.

The second section is called "Problem Solving." These questions are more challenging. The answer may not be found just by reading the lesson. You may have to think harder.

The third section is called "Skills." In this section you will be asked to read tables and graphs.

Metric Measurement

In this book you will learn about measuring many different things. These things are measured in units of the metric system. To help you understand the metric system, look at the following drawings. Then look around your home and school for other things that are measured in metric units.

TEMPERATURE

100°C—water boils —100°
—90°
—80°
—70°
—60°
—50°
37°C—normal body —40°
temperature —30°
—20°
—10°
0°C—water freezes —0°

LENGTH

5 cm

this large paper clip is
5 centimeters (cm) long

VOLUME

4 milk cartons contain
about 1 liter (L) of milk

1 teaspoon equals 5 milliliters (mL)

about 100 m

1 football field is about 100 meters (m) long
10 football fields placed end to end are about 1 kilometer (km) long

MASS

2 small paper clips have a
mass of about 1 gram (g)

an apple has a mass of
about 40 grams (g)

Bb
Encyclopedia

an encyclopedia book has
a mass of about
1 kilogram (kg)

Chapter 1

Animals

LESSON QUESTIONS

Animals and Their Young (pp. 4–6)

1. How are the eggs of turtles different from those of birds?
2. Name an animal that may lay only one egg a year. Name another animal that may lay many eggs at one time.
3. How do mammals feed their young when they are born?

Animals Grow and Change (pp. 8–12)

1. Why do many insects lay their eggs on leaves?

2. Name the stages of growth of the butterfly shown in the pictures.
3. How is a butterfly larva different from a butterfly pupa?
4. How is a grasshopper nymph different from a grasshopper adult?

Caring for the Young (pp. 13–17)

1. Name some newborn animals that do not need care after they are born.
2. What skills do mammals such as bear cubs and lion cubs learn from their parents?

PROBLEM SOLVING

Use after page 7. The eggs of most birds are oval in shape. They are narrower at one end than at the other end. How does this oval shape solve a problem for parent birds?

Use after page 7. Inside the egg where a young chick is growing, there is an air space. Predict what might happen if an egg had no air space.

Reading a Bar Graph

A bar graph can be used to show and compare information. This bar graph shows the number of eggs laid by different kinds of birds in one year. Use the bar graph to answer these questions.

1. Which of these birds lays the most eggs in one year?

2. Which lays the fewest eggs in one year?

3. Which birds lay more eggs than a blue jay in one year?

4. How many more eggs does a partridge lay than a robin?

5. How many fewer eggs does a gull lay than a mallard duck?

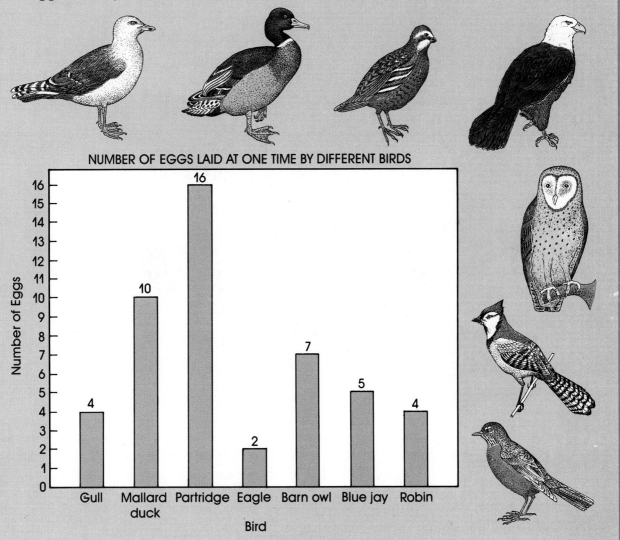

NUMBER OF EGGS LAID AT ONE TIME BY DIFFERENT BIRDS

Number of Eggs

Bird	Gull	Mallard duck	Partridge	Eagle	Barn owl	Blue jay	Robin
Number of Eggs	4	10	16	2	7	5	4

Chapter 2

Animals Are Important

LESSON QUESTIONS

Food from Animals (pp. 22–24)

1. Name three foods we get from animals.
2. What is poultry? What food comes from poultry?

People Raise Other Animals (pp. 25–28)

1. Where does down come from? Where is down used?
2. Where does wool come from? Where is wool used?
3. What materials are these items made of? What animals did the materials come from?

A

B

4. Describe two ways animals help people.

Endangered Animals (pp. 29–33)

1. What is an endangered animal?
2. Describe two ways animals become endangered.
3. How have these animals become endangered?

A

B

Animals Need People (pp. 34–35)

1. What does *extinct* mean?
2. What is a wildlife refuge? Why are wildlife refuges important?

PROBLEM SOLVING

Use after page 35. In a wildlife refuge the animals are not kept in cages. How, then, does a wildlife refuge keep animals like birds and ducks inside when they are free to fly away?

Reading a Table

This table shows many examples of endangered animals. The table also explains how the animals became endangered. Use the table to answer the following questions.

1. How did mountain gorillas become endangered?
2. How did North Atlantic salmon become endangered?
3. Which of the animals became endangered because they were captured for zoos and research?
4. Which of the animals became endangered because of hunting?
5. Which of these animals are birds? How did each of these birds become endangered?

ENDANGERED ANIMALS

Animal	What Caused It to Become Endangered
Mountain gorilla	Forests in which they live have been destroyed by people
Bald eagle	Pesticides
California condor	Hunting
Orangutan	Captured for zoos and research
Puffin	Oil spills
Polar bear	Hunting
North Atlantic salmon	Water pollution
Bengal tiger	Hunting
Giant anteater	Captured for zoos and research

Chapter 3

Seed Plants

LESSON QUESTIONS

Roots (pp. 40–42)
1. Why are roots important?
2. What is a taproot?
3. Describe a fibrous root.
4. Describe a prop root.

Stems (pp. 43–47)
1. Why are stems important?
2. Describe a tree stem.
3. Describe a shrub stem.
4. Give two examples of plants that have vines.

Leaves (pp. 48–50)
1. What three things do leaves need to make food?
2. Where do plants get the things they need to make food?

Flowers and Seeds (pp. 51–56)
1. Where do seeds form?
2. What is a seed coat?
3. What happens when a seed germinates?

PROBLEM SOLVING

Use after page 47. Why are tomato plants often held up by wooden stakes?

Use after page 50. Pretend you are a scientist who is going to live on a strange planet. The planet has very little oxygen in the air. Instead the air is mostly carbon dioxide. Make a plan for putting more oxygen into the air.

Use after page 50. Suppose you wanted to do an experiment to find out how fast bean plants grow. You would record their exact height every hour of the day for 10 days. During which hours of the day do you think the plants would grow most? Explain your answer.

Use after page 56. Many fruits can float. Some, like the coconut, can float for long distances. Coconuts grow on islands that are surrounded by water. How does a floating seed help a coconut?

Use after page 56. How could you identify a strange seed? Describe three different things you could do.

SKILLS

Reading a Diagram

Some diagrams show a lot of information. The drawings in this diagram show eight trees and shrubs. The drawings show how tall each tree and shrub usually is after 15 years. Use the diagram to answer these questions.

1. Which of these trees is the tallest after 15 years?

2. Which of these trees is the smallest after 15 years?
3. After 15 years, how much taller is a Douglas fir than an oak?
4. Which is usually taller after 15 years, a yew or a poplar?
5. After 15 years, how much shorter is a yew than a silver birch?

| Juniper | Yew | Oak | Poplar | Weeping willow | Silver birch | Douglas fir |
| 3 meters | 4 meters | 8 meters | 9 meters | 9 meters | 9 meters | 12 meters |

HEIGHTS OF 15-YEAR-OLD TREES

297

Chapter 4

Plants Are Important

LESSON QUESTIONS

Food from Plants (pp. 62–69)

1. What is the stored food in plants called? Where is food stored in plants?
2. What are grains? Name three grains.
3. Name four examples of foods that you get from plants.
4. Name a plant used for food that is not a green plant.
5. What parts of these green plants are used as food?

Other Uses of Plants (pp. 70–74)

1. How are plants used for decoration?

2. What is compost? How is it useful?
3. Name a medicine that is made from plants.
4. Name two products that come from trees.

Harmful Plants (pp. 75–76)

1. What is mildew? How is it harmful?
2. Describe three harmful plants. Tell what the harmful part of each plant is. Tell how the plant is harmful.

A

B

C

D

PROBLEM SOLVING

Use after page 74. Some people do not live near a store that sells gardening supplies. How can these people get seeds, stakes, and fertilizer? How can they control insects?

Use after page 76. Scientists who study plants know which ones are harmful. How do you think they learned which ones are not safe to eat?

Use after page 76. Why does mildew often form on damp towels at the bottom of a full laundry basket? What could be done to prevent this from happening?

Use after page 76. Why is the growth of mold and mildew a bigger problem in summer than in winter?

Reading a Pictograph

A pictograph is an easy way to show information. In a pictograph, pictures are used as symbols. This pictograph shows how many apples a farmer picked in 5 days. Each apple is a symbol that stands for 10 apples.

Use the graph to answer these questions.

1. How many apples were picked on Tuesday?

2. On which day were the most apples picked?

3. On which day were the fewest apples picked?

4. How many more apples were picked on Monday than on Friday?

5. How many apples were picked during the 5 days?

NUMBER OF APPLES PICKED

Monday	🍎🍎🍎🍎🍎🍎🍎🍎🍎
Tuesday	🍎🍎🍎🍎🍎🍎
Wednesday	🍎🍎🍎🍎
Thursday	🍎🍎🍎🍎🍎🍎🍎
Friday	🍎🍎🍎

🍎 = 10 apples

Chapter 5

All About Matter

LESSON QUESTIONS

Properties of Matter (pp. 88–90)
1. What is anything that takes up space and has mass called?
2. What is a balance?

States of Matter (pp. 91–93)
1. What are the three states of matter?
2. Describe the properties of a solid.
3. Give an example of a liquid. What properties do all liquids have in common?

The Particles in Matter (pp. 94–95)
1. What is an atom?

2. Describe the particles that make up each of the objects below–air, water, and metal.

Matter Can Change (pp. 96–98)
1. What is a physical change? Give an example of a physical change.
2. At what temperature does water turn to ice? What is this point called?
3. What is evaporation?
4. How is evaporation different from condensation?

Different Kinds of Matter (pp. 99–101)
1. What is a chemical change?
2. Give two examples of chemical changes.

A   B   C

PROBLEM SOLVING

Use after page 90. Scientists choose their words very carefully. Why are words like *mass, solid, liquid,* and *gas* important words to scientists?

Use after page 90. Suppose you did not have a scale or a balance. How could you compare the masses of two objects?

Use after page 98. What state of matter is in a cloud? How can the matter that forms clouds change from one state to another?

Use after page 98. How can changing states of water be a problem for people?

SKILLS

Reading a Diagram
This diagram shows the temperatures of different kinds of things. Use the diagram to answer the following questions.

1. At what temperature does water freeze?

2. What is normal human body temperature?

3. How much greater is the temperature at which water boils than normal room temperature?
4. How much less is the body temperature of a yellow perch than the body temperature of a human?
5. Do you think the lowest temperature ever recorded in North America is higher or lower than 2°C? Explain your answer.

TEMPERATURES

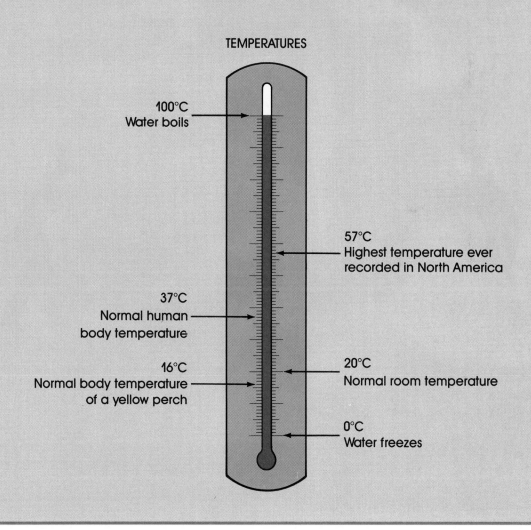

100°C
Water boils

57°C
Highest temperature ever
recorded in North America

37°C
Normal human
body temperature

16°C
Normal body temperature
of a yellow perch

20°C
Normal room temperature

0°C
Water freezes

Chapter 6

Force, Work, and Energy

LESSON QUESTIONS

Forces (pp. 106–108)

1. What is a force?
2. When would you use a greater force–when you lift a book or when you lift a piece of paper?
3. What do forces do?

Kinds of Forces (pp. 109–114)

1. What is gravity? What does gravity do to objects on the earth?
2. What is magnetism? Is magnetism a pushing force or a pulling force?
3. What force slows down or stops motion? How can you reduce this force?

Work (pp. 115–116)

1. What is work?
2. What does the amount of work that is done depend on?
3. Which of the pictures below show no work being done?

Energy (pp. 117–119)

1. What is energy? Name four kinds of energy.
2. Name two ways electricity can be used to do work.

PROBLEM SOLVING

Use after page 108. Are forces a form of matter? Why or why not?

Use after page 114. Can friction be a useful force? Why are people who design shoes and who make tires interested in increasing friction?

Use after page 116. Which is more work?
a. Running up 10 steps as fast as you can
b. Walking up 10 steps slowly

SKILLS

Reading a Pictograph

This pictograph shows the masses of many different things. The symbol is used to stand for 10 kilograms of mass. Use the pictograph to answer the following questions.

1. What is the mass of a raccoon?
2. What is the mass of a polar bear?
3. How much greater is the mass of a coyote than the mass of a chicken?
4. How much less is the mass of a bicycle than the mass of a man?
5. Do you think a skateboard has a mass that is greater than or less than 13 kilograms? Explain your answer.

EXAMPLES OF COMMON MASSES

Polar bear — 322 kilograms

Bicycle — 13 kilograms

Adult man — 73 kilograms

Chicken — 3 kilograms

Raccoon — 10 kilograms

Coyote — 34 kilograms

= 10 kilograms

303

Chapter 7

Machines

LESSON QUESTIONS

The Lever—A Simple Machine (pp. 124–127)
1. What is a machine? Give two examples of machines.
2. What is a lever? How are levers used to do work?
3. When using a lever, what is the load and what is the force?
4. Name two examples of levers.

Using an Inclined Plane (pp. 128–131)
1. How can an inclined plane be used to do work?
2. What is a wedge? What can a wedge be used to do?
3. Tell how a screw is an inclined plane.

The Wheel and Axle (pp. 132–134)
1. What is a wheel and axle made of? Give an example of a wheel and axle.
2. What is a gear? Where are gears used?

Pulleys (pp. 135–137)
1. What is a pulley? Name a place a pulley can be used.
2. How is a fixed pulley different from a movable pulley?

Compound Machines (pp. 138–139)
1. What is a compound machine?
2. Name two examples of compound machines.

PROBLEM SOLVING

Use after page 127. Look at the lever below. How can you change the lever to reduce the force needed to lift the load? How could you change the lever so that you push down less distance to move the load a greater distance?

Use after page 139. Look at the compound machine. Name the simple machines that make up the compound machine and tell how each helps to do work.

304

Reading a Bar Graph

A group of third graders held a contest. They wanted to see who could lift the most weight with a pulley. The results of the contest are shown below in the bar graph. Use the bar graph to answer the following questions.

1. Which of the children was able to lift the most?

2. Which of the children lifted the least?

3. How much more did Michael lift than Jenny did?

4. Which of the children lifted more than 6 kilograms?

5. Which of the children lifted less than Joe lifted?

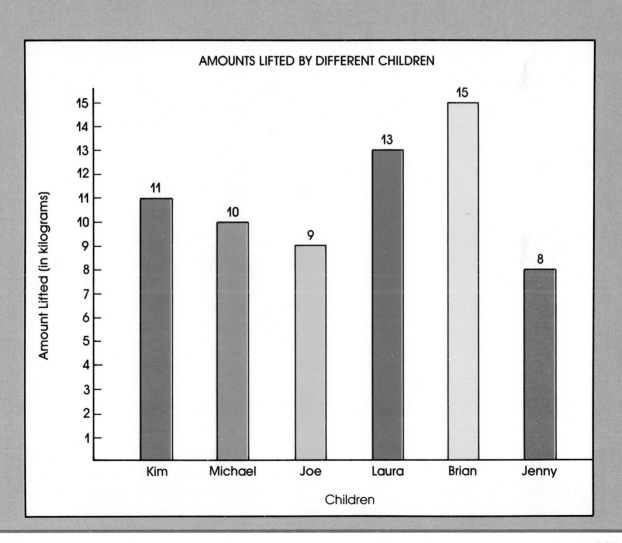

AMOUNTS LIFTED BY DIFFERENT CHILDREN

Chapter 8

Sound

LESSON QUESTIONS

Making Sound (pp. 144–145)
1. Where does sound come from?
2. How does sound move through matter?

Different Sounds (pp. 146–148)
1. What is volume?
2. What is pitch? Give an example of something with a high pitch. Give an example of something with a low pitch.
3. Rank the instruments shown below by pitch (1-highest and 4-lowest).

How Sound Moves (pp. 149–151)
1. How is the way sound moves through gases different from the way it moves through solids?

2. When does sound travel faster—when it moves through water or when it moves through rock?

How Sound Bounces (pp. 152–153)
1. How does sound reflect from a smooth surface? From a rough surface?
2. What is an echo?

Sounds Made by Living Things (pp. 154–157)
1. What are vocal cords? What are vocal cords used for?
2. Name two animals that use sound to locate objects.

A   B

C   D

PROBLEM SOLVING

Use after page 148. How many different sounds can you make using only a piece of paper? Try to make at least 10 sounds.

Use after page 148. Why, do you think, is the sound of fingernails scratching a chalkboard unpleasant to some people but not to others?

Use after page 151. Design an experiment to prove that sound moves better through some things than it does through others.

Reading a Table

A table is a list of facts. This table shows the speed of sound through different materials. Use the table to answer the following questions.

1. How fast does sound travel through salt water?
2. How fast does sound travel through wax?
3. Through which material does sound travel faster–air at room temperature or cork?
4. Through which material does sound travel slower–air at room temperature or air at 100°C?
5. How much faster does air travel through wax than through cork?

SPEED OF SOUND IN MATTER

Matter	Speed (in meters per second)
Air at room temperature	340
Air at 100°C	386
Cork	500
Salt water	1470
Wax	880

Chapter 9

The Changing Earth

PROBLEM SOLVING

Use after page 178. Icebergs are mountains of ice that float in water. Why, do you think, are they not round and smooth like the rocks in a stream?

Use after page 178. Explain why many roads are in poor condition after a hard winter.

Use after page 180. You live next to a desert. Winds constantly blow sand into your house. Make a plan to prevent this from happening.

Use after page 183. Many workers make their living by digging into the earth's crust. Name three jobs that depend on the earth's crust.

Reading a Diagram

One way we know about the inside of the earth is by drilling into it. This diagram shows the deepest drilling ever done in five states. Use the diagram to answer the following questions.

1. How deep was the deepest drilling ever done in Texas?
2. How deep was the deepest drilling ever done in Louisiana?
3. In which of the states shown here was the deepest drilling ever done?
4. How much deeper was the deepest drilling ever done in Oklahoma than the deepest drilling ever done in California?
5. The deepest drilling ever done in the world was 9733 meters deep. How much deeper is this than the deepest drilling ever done in Texas?

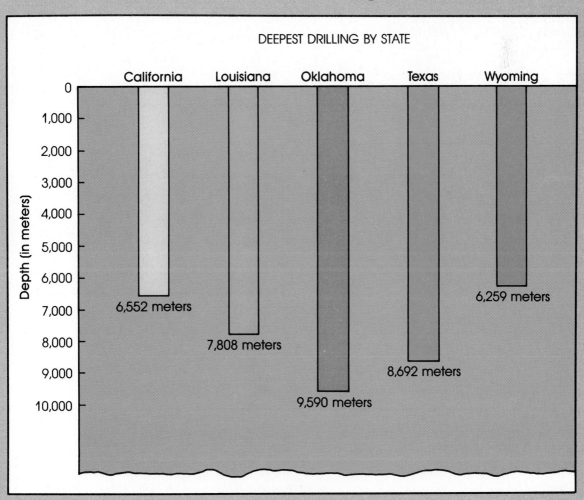

DEEPEST DRILLING BY STATE

California — 6,552 meters
Louisiana — 7,808 meters
Oklahoma — 9,590 meters
Texas — 8,692 meters
Wyoming — 6,259 meters

Depth (in meters)

Chapter 10

The Earth's Resources

LESSON QUESTIONS

Soil as a Resource (pp. 188–190)
1. What is a natural resource? Give two examples of natural resources.
2. Why is soil important?
3. What materials make up soil?

The Air Around Us (pp. 191-194)
1. Name two ways wind can be useful.
2. What is the atmosphere? Name two gases found in the atmosphere.
3. What is pollution?

The Earth's Water Supply (pp. 195–197)
1. Why is water an important resource?
2. What is a reservoir?
3. What is irrigation? Why is it important?

Energy from the Earth (pp. 198–199)
1. What is a fuel?
2. Why are coal, oil, and gas important? How were coal, oil, and gas formed?

Some Other Resources (pp. 200–201)
1. Name three metals that are found in rocks.
2. What are gems? How are gems used?
3. How are the natural resources shown below used?

marble

diamond   metal ore

PROBLEM SOLVING

Use after page 190. Tell why you would not expect to find much humus in a desert. In what kind of place would you expect to find a lot of humus?

Use after page 199. Suppose you found an unknown substance in the earth's crust. It looked like oil. It smelled like oil. How could you tell if this substance was a new fuel?

Reading a Map

Sometimes, maps can be used to show where resources are. This map shows the resources found in Indiana. There is a different symbol for each resource shown on the map. Use the map to answer the following questions.

1. What plant resources are shown on this map?
2. What other resources are shown?
3. Find South Bend. What plant resources are found near South Bend?
4. What plant resources are found in the southwestern, or bottom left, part of Indiana?
5. Where is oil found in Indiana?
6. Find Terre Haute. What resources are found near Terre Haute?

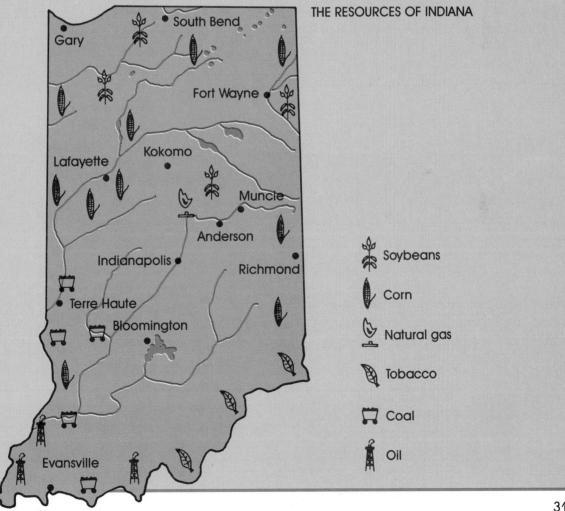

THE RESOURCES OF INDIANA

Soybeans
Corn
Natural gas
Tobacco
Coal
Oil

Chapter 11

The Weather Around You

LESSON QUESTIONS

Heating the Earth (pp. 206–207)
1. What happens to sunlight that strikes the earth?
2. How is the earth like a giant heater?

Seasons (pp. 208–210)
1. How does the sun strike the earth in the winter? How is this different from the way it strikes the earth in the summer?
2. What causes the change of seasons?

Heating Different Surfaces (pp. 211–212)
1. How does land heat and cool? How is this different from the way water heats and cools?
2. Why is the air in polar regions cold?
3. What causes wind?

Water in the Air (pp. 213–214)
1. How does energy from the sun change water in lakes, rivers, and oceans?
2. Name two things that speed up the evaporation of water.
3. How is dew different from frost?

Clouds (pp. 215–217)
1. How are clouds formed?
2. Describe three kinds of clouds.
3. Describe three kinds of precipitation.

Water Cycle (pp. 218–220)
1. What three things might happen to water that falls onto land?
2. Describe the water cycle.

PROBLEM SOLVING

Use after page 207. On a hot day, why is it cooler to walk on grass than on a sidewalk? On a snowy day, why does snow collect on grass first?

Use after page 212. In cold places, bridges often have a sign that reads "Bridge freezes before roadway." Why, do you think, does water on a bridge freeze first?

Use after page 214. In winter many people use a humidifier in their home. The humidifier sprays a mist of water into the air. What problem does this solve?

Use after page 220. What would happen to the water cycle if oil covered the oceans?

Reading a Bar Graph

This bar graph shows the amount of rain that fell in one year in a city. Use the bar graph to answer the following questions.

1. In which month or months did the most rain fall?
2. In which month or months did the least amount of rain fall?
3. How much rain fell during April?
4. How much rain fell during December?
5. How much more rain fell during August than during November?
6. During which half of the year did the most rain fall, during the first half or during the second half?

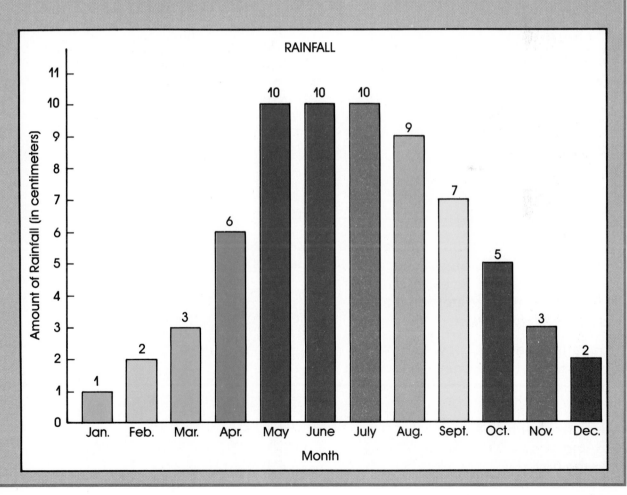

Chapter 12

Sun, Moon, and Planets

LESSON QUESTIONS

Looking at the Moon and the Sun (pp. 226–229)

1. Why does the moon look larger than the sun?
2. What is the surface of the moon like?
3. What is a crater?
4. What is the sun like?

Motions in Space (pp. 230–231)

1. What is a satellite? What satellite has always moved around the earth?
2. What is a revolution? How long does it take the earth to make one revolution?
3. What is a rotation? How long does it take the earth to make one rotation?

Phases of the Moon (pp. 232–233)

1. What is a phase?
2. Describe the full moon phase.
3. Describe the new moon phase.

Eclipses (pp. 234–236)

1. What is an eclipse?
2. What causes an eclipse of the moon?
3. What causes an eclipse of the sun?

The Planets (pp. 237–239)

1. What planets make up the solar system?
2. Which planet is closest to the sun? Which is the farthest from the sun?

PROBLEM SOLVING

Use after page 229. You have learned that the moon has craters. Long ago, space rocks also hit the earth, causing craters. How might craters on the earth be different from those on the moon?

Use after page 233. Draw four phases of the moon that will never be seen on the earth.

Use after page 233. One half of the lighted side of the moon can be seen during first and last quarters. Explain how the moon is different in these two quarters.

Use after page 236. Eclipses of the moon and sun were often frightening to people who lived long ago. Why, do you suppose, were they afraid?

Use after page 239. In 1979, Pluto moved closer to the sun than Neptune did. Pluto will be closer than Neptune for the next 20 years. In what ways will these two planets be different for the next 20 years?

SKILLS

Reading a Table
This table lists the planets. The table also shows the time it takes for each planet to orbit the sun and the number of satellites each planet has.

Use the table to answer these questions.
1. How long does it take the earth to make one orbit?
2. Which planet has the shortest orbit?
3. Suppose you went to Saturn today. How old would you be after one orbit was made?
4. Which planet has as many satellites as the earth has?
5. How many more satellites does Jupiter have than Neptune has?

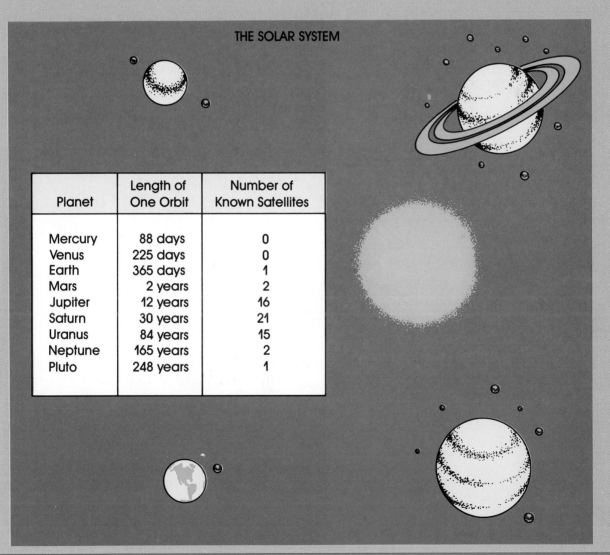

THE SOLAR SYSTEM

Planet	Length of One Orbit	Number of Known Satellites
Mercury	88 days	0
Venus	225 days	0
Earth	365 days	1
Mars	2 years	2
Jupiter	12 years	16
Saturn	30 years	21
Uranus	84 years	15
Neptune	165 years	2
Pluto	248 years	1

315

Good Health Habits

LESSON QUESTIONS

Keeping Yourself Clean (pp. 250–253)
1. What is a habit?
2. Describe three good health habits for keeping clean.

Teeth Care (pp. 254–256)
1. What is plaque? Why is it important to remove plaque?
2. What is a hole in a tooth called?
3. Describe two ways to help care for your teeth.

Exercise and Sleep (pp. 257–260)
1. Why is exercise important to your health?
2. Describe three ways you can get exercise.
3. Why is sleep important to your health?

Safety Habits (pp. 261–263)
1. Describe four rules you should follow when riding a bicycle.
2. How can you prevent bicycle accidents?
3. What do each of the following hand signals mean?

A   B

PROBLEM SOLVING

Use after page 260. Have you ever slept in someone else's house? Why is it sometimes more difficult to sleep in a new place? How can you solve this problem?

Use after page 263. Scientists do experiments to learn how people see colors. These show that lighter colors are seen more easily at night than darker ones. How have people used this fact in teaching safety habits?

Reading a Table

Your normal body temperature is 37°C. Other living things have body temperatures that are higher or lower than yours. Some of these living things are shown in this table. Use it to answer the following questions.

1. Which of these animals has the highest body temperature?
2. Which of these animals has a higher body temperature than you do?
3. Which of these animals has the lowest body temperature?
4. Which of these animals are birds? What is the body temperature of each of these birds?
5. How much higher is the body temperature of a horned lizard than the body temperature of a mole salamander?

BODY TEMPERATURES OF DIFFERENT ANIMALS

Animal	Normal Body Temperature
Arctic gull	34°C
Blue jay	43°C
Goat	40°C
Horned lizard	35°C
House sparrow	41°C
Largemouth bass	24°C
Mole salamander	17°C
Yellow perch	16°C

Chapter 14

Nutrition

LESSON QUESTIONS

The Need for Food (pp. 268–269)
1. Why is food important?
2. Name three foods that have a lot of energy.

Kinds of Foods (pp. 270–274)
1. Name the six main kinds of nutrients.
2. Name three foods that contain starch. Why is starch important?
3. Why is protein important?
4. Name three places you can get water everyday.

5. Name a nutrient found in each of the foods shown below.

Food Groups (pp. 275–278)
1. What is a diet?
2. What does a balanced diet include?
3. Name four items in the meat group.
4. Name four items in the milk group.

Healthy Eating Habits (pp. 279–281)
1. Describe two healthy snacks.
2. Describe two healthy eating habits.

A

B

C

D

E

Honey

F

PROBLEM SOLVING

Use after page 269. Long-distance runners eat a lot of bread, potatoes, and spaghetti-type foods on the days before a race. Why, do you think, do they do this?

Use after page 281. Have you ever heard the saying, "An apple a day keeps the doctor away"? What does this saying really mean? Why is eating apples a good health habit?

Reading a Graph

The graph shown here is a bar graph. It shows the heights of students. The graph also shows how many students are the same height.

Use the graph to answer these questions.

1. The most students are what height?
2. The fewest students are what height?
3. How many students are 126 centimeters tall?
4. What is the difference in height between the tallest student and the shortest student?

HEIGHTS OF THIRD GRADERS

Number of students

Height (in centimeters)

Glossary

Key to Pronunciation

a apple, bat	i if, pig	sh she, wish	ə stands for:
ā ate, page	ī idea, fine	th think, moth	a in asleep
ã air, care	ng ring, sink	ᵮн the, bathe	e in garden
ä father, star	o ox, top	u uncle, sun	i in pencil
ch chest, such	ō owe, no	u̇ pull, foot	o in button
e egg, bed	ô orbit, saw	ü glue, boot	u in circus
ē even, me	oi oil, joy	zh usual, vision	
ėr earn, bird	ou out, mouse		

This Key to Pronunciation is adapted from *Scott, Foresman Intermediate Dictionary,* by E. L. Thorndike and Clarence L. Barnhart. Copyright © 1983 by Scott, Foresman and Company. Reprinted by permission.

adult   The final stage in the growth of animals. *p. 10*

atmosphere (at′mə sfir)   The layer of air that surrounds the earth. *p. 193*

atom (at′əm)   The smallest particle that makes up matter. *p. 94*

balance (bal′əns)   A tool used to measure mass. *p. 89*

boiling point   The temperature at which water begins to boil (100°C). *p. 97*

carbon dioxide (kär′bən   dī ok′sīd)   A gas found in the air. Plants use carbon dioxide to make food. *p. 48*

cavity (kav′ə tē)   A hole in the outside covering of a tooth that is caused by decay. *p. 255*

chemical change   When one kind of matter becomes a different kind of matter. *p. 99*

cloud   Millions of tiny water drops that form when water vapor collects on bits of dust. *p. 215*

communication (kə myü nə kā′shən)   The sending of messages. *p. 154*

compost (kom′pōst)   A mixture made of rotted plant materials. Compost is used to restore minerals to the soil. *p. 71*

compound machine   A machine that is made of two or more simple machines. *p. 138*

condensation (kon den sā′shən)   The change from a gas to a liquid. *p. 98*

core (kôr)   The layer of the earth under the mantle. The core is the hottest part of the earth. *p. 169*

crater (krā′tər) A bowl-shaped area found on the surface of the moon. *p. 228*

crust (krust) The outer layer of the earth. The crust is mostly solid rock. *p. 168*

dental floss (flôs) A special kind of thread that is used to clean teeth. *p. 255*

dew Drops of water that form when water vapor in the air touches cool objects. *p. 214*

diet (dī′ət) All the food you eat. *p. 275*

down Soft feathers from birds such as ducks and geese. *p. 25*

earthquake (ėrth′kwāk) A movement of the layers of rock in the earth's crust. *p. 171*

echo (ek′ō) A sound that bounces back after it hits an object. *p. 153*

eclipse (i klips′) The effect produced when one body in space passes into the shadow of another body in space. *p. 234*

eclipse of the moon A darkening of the moon as it passes into the earth's shadow. *p. 235*

eclipse of the sun A darkening of the sun as the moon passes between the sun and the earth. *p. 235*

egg The first stage of growth of some kinds of animals. The egg contains everything needed to form a new animal. *p. 9*

endangered (en dān′jərd) When only a few of a certain kind of plant or animal remain. *p. 29*

energy The ability to do work. *p. 117*

erosion (i rō′zhən) The movement of rock, sand, or soil by water or wind. *p. 175*

evaporation (i vap ə rā′shən) The change from a liquid to a gas. *p. 98*

extinct (ek stingkt′) When a kind of plant or animal is gone forever. *p. 34*

fat One of the six main kinds of nutrients your body needs. *p. 271*

fibrous (fī′brəs) **root** One of many small roots. Fibrous roots are all about the same size. *p. 41*

fixed pulley A pulley that stays in one place when it is being used. *p. 136*

force (fôrs) A push or a pull that is needed to make something move. *p. 106*

freezing point The temperature at which water begins to freeze (0°C). *p. 97*

friction (frik′shən)   A kind of force that slows down or stops motion. *p. 113*

frost   Ice crystals that form when water vapor freezes on objects. *p. 214*

fuel   A material that can be broken down to release energy. *p. 198*

gas   A state of matter. A gas always has the same shape as the container it fills. *p. 91*

gear   A kind of simple machine that is like a wheel and axle. A gear is a wheel with teeth. *p. 134*

gem (jem)   A beautiful mineral, such as a diamond, that is sometimes found in a rock. *p. 201*

germ (jėrm)   A tiny living thing that can make people sick. *p. 250*

germinate (jėr′mə nāt)   To grow from a seed into a new plant. *p. 55*

grain (grān)   A seed from certain grasses, such as oats, wheat, rice, and corn. *p. 65*

gravity (grav′ə tē)   The force of one object pulling on another object. Gravity pulls things toward the earth. *p. 109*

habit (hab′it)   Something that can be done without thinking. *p. 250*

herb (ėrb)   A kind of seed plant that is small and has a soft stem. *p. 46*

hide   The skin of animals such as cattle, sheep, and pigs. *p. 26*

humus (hyü′məs)   Bits of plant and animal matter found in soil. Humus returns useful materials to the soil. *p. 189*

inclined (in klīnd′) **plane**   A kind of simple machine. An inclined plane is a slanted surface that makes it easier to move an object to a higher place. *p. 128*

irrigation (ir ə gā′shən)   The watering of crops when there is not enough rain. *p. 196*

larva (lär′və)   The second stage of growth of some kinds of insects. *p. 9*

lava (lä′və)   Melted rock that flows from a volcano. *p. 173*

lever (lev′ər)   A kind of simple machine used to lift or move things. *p. 125*

liquid (lik′wid)   A state of matter. A liquid always has the same shape as its container. *p. 91*

load   The object to be lifted or moved by a machine. *p. 125*

lubricant (lü′brə kənt)   A substance, such as oil or grease, that reduces friction. *p. 114*

machine   Any tool that can help people to do work. *p. 124*

magma (mag′mə) Melted rock that is inside the earth's crust. *p. 172*

magnetism (mag′nə tiz əm) A force that acts on some kinds of metals. *p. 112*

mammal (mam′əl) An animal that has hair and feeds its young with mother's milk. *p. 6*

mantle (man′təl) The layer of the earth that lies beneath the crust. The mantle is made of rocklike material. *p. 169*

mass The measure of how much matter there is in an object. *p. 89*

matter Anything that takes up space and has mass. *p. 88*

mildew (mil′dü) A kind of nongreen plant that grows in shady, damp places. *p. 75*

minerals One of the six main kinds of nutrients your body needs. *p. 272*

movable pulley A pulley that moves as a load is moved. *p. 136*

natural resources (nach′ər əl ri sôr′siz) Useful materials that come from the earth. *p. 188*

nutrient (nü′trē ənts) The part of food that helps a person grow and gives energy. *p. 270*

nymph (nimf) The second stage of growth of some kinds of insects. A nymph is like a tiny adult without wings. *p. 11*

orbit (ôr′bit) The path a satellite follows. *p. 230*

ore (ôr) A rock that contains metal. *p. 200*

oxygen (ok′sə jən) A gas found in the air. Plants give off oxygen. Most living things need oxygen to stay alive. *p. 49*

phase (fāz) A change in the way the moon looks when it is seen from the earth. *p. 232*

physical (fiz′ə kəl) **change** Any change in the size, shape, or state of matter. *p. 96*

pitch The highness or lowness of sound. *p. 147*

planet (plan′it) A body that revolves around the sun. There are nine planets in the solar system. *p. 237*

plaque (plak) A sticky film that forms on the surfaces of teeth. Plaque can cause teeth to decay. *p. 255*

pollution (pə lü′shən) Anything dirty in the earth's water or air. *p. 193*

poultry (pōl′trē)   Birds such as chickens and turkeys that are used for food. *p. 23*

precipitation (pri sip ə tā′shən)   Water that falls in the form of rain, hail, snow, or sleet. *p. 217*

prop roots   Extra roots that grow out from the sides of stems. *p. 42*

protein (prō′tēn)   One of the six main kinds of nutrients your body needs. *p. 271*

pulley (pül′ē)   A kind of simple machine. A pulley is a wheel with a rope around it. It is used to move objects to places that are hard to reach. *p. 135*

pupa (pyü′pə)   The third stage of growth of some kinds of insects. A pupa lives inside a hard covering. *p. 9*

reflected sound   A sound that has changed the direction of its movement. *p. 152*

reservoir (rez′ər vwär)   A place where water is stored. *p. 196*

revolution (rev ə lü′shən)   The motion of the earth and the moon in their orbits. *p. 231*

rotation (rō tā′shən)   The spinning motion of some bodies in space. *p. 231*

satellite (sat′ə līt)   A body in space that moves around a larger body. *p. 230*

screw   A kind of simple machine that is like an inclined plane wrapped around a center post. *p. 130*

seed coat   A seed covering. *p. 54*

shrub   A kind of seed plant that is smaller than a tree and has many woody stems. *p. 45*

simple machine   A machine with few or no moving parts. *p. 124*

sleet   Frozen drops of rain. *p. 217*

snowflakes   Ice crystals that form from water vapor when the temperature in a cloud is below freezing. *p. 217*

solar system (sō′lər sis′təm)   The sun and the planets that revolve around it. *p. 237*

solid   A state of matter. A solid always has a shape of its own. *p. 91*

starch (stärch)   Food stored in the seeds, roots, stems, and leaves of green plants. *p. 62*   One of the six main kinds of nutrients your body needs. *p. 270*

sugar   One of the six main kinds of nutrients your body needs. *p. 270*

sun flare   A giant stream of glowing gas that explodes from the surface of the sun. *p. 229*

taproot   A large main root. *p. 41*

topsoil   The top layer of soil. *p. 189*

tree   A kind of seed plant that has one main stem called a trunk. *p. 45*

vibration (vī brā′shən)   The back-and-forth movement of matter. Some vibrations cause sound. *p. 144*

vine   A kind of seed plant that has soft stems and climbs as it grows. *p. 47*

vitamins (vī′tə mins)   One of the six main kinds of nutrients your body needs. *p. 272*

vocal (vō′kəl) **cords**   Special flaps of muscle found in the throat. They move back and forth to make sounds in the throat. *p. 154*

volcano (vol kā′nō)   An opening in the earth's crust through which hot melted rock flows. *p. 172*

volume (vol′yəm)   The loudness or softness of sound. *p. 146*

water   One of the six main kinds of nutrients your body needs. *p. 273*

water cycle (sī′kəl)   The change in the state of water that happens over and over again. *p. 218*

water vapor (vā′pər)   Water in the form of a gas. *p. 96*

weathering (weẗH′ər ing)   The wearing away and breaking of rock by moving water and wind. *p. 174*

wedge (wej)   A kind of simple machine formed by two inclined planes. *p. 129*

wheel and axle (ak′səl)   A kind of simple machine that is made of a wheel that turns on a center post. *p. 132*

wildlife refuge (wīld′līf ref′yüj)   A safe place were wild animals live. *p. 34*

wind   Moving air. *p. 212*

work   The use of a force to move something. *p. 115*

Index

Credits

Rotker/Taurus Photos; *b.* © Lawrence Migdale/Photo Researchers, Inc.; *inset* Holt Confer/Grant Heilman Photography. 73: *t.* Grant Heilman Photography; *m.* © Bruce Roberts/Photo Researchers, Inc.; *b.* Silver Burdett & Ginn. 74: *t.l., m.l.* Silver Burdett & Ginn; *b.l.* © Brian Brake/Photo Researchers, Inc.; *t.r.* Vance Henry/Taurus Photos; *inset* Hickson-Bender for Silver Burdett & Ginn. 75: *t.* D. Lyons/Bruce Coleman; *b.* © Russ Kinne/Photo Researchers, Inc. 77: Dan De Wilde for Silver Burdett & Ginn. 80: *l.* © Charles Belinky/Photo Researchers, Inc.; *t.r.* © Kent and Donna Dannen/Photo Researchers, Inc.; © Larry Mulvehill/Photo Researchers, Inc.; *b.* Leonard Lee Rue/Bruce Coleman.

Unit Two 84: *t.* Pat Field/Bruce Coleman; *b.* David Madison/Bruce Coleman. 85: *l.* Bruce Curtis/Peter Arnold, Inc.; *r.* Leonore Weber/Taurus Photos.

Chapter 5 86–87: Silver Burdett & Ginn. 88: *l.* Silver Burdett & Ginn; *r.* Dan De Wilde for Silver Burdett & Ginn. 89: Silver Burdett & Ginn. 90: Dan De Wilde for Silver Burdett & Ginn. 91–93: Silver Burdett & Ginn. 95: *b.* Dan De Wilde for Silver Burdett & Ginn. 96: *l.* Silver Burdett & Ginn; *r.* Dan De Wilde for Silver Burdett & Ginn. 97: *l.* Isaac Geib/Grant Heilman Photography; *r.* Larry P. Harris/Tom Stack & Associates. 98, 99: Silver Burdett & Ginn. 100: Dan De Wilde for Silver Burdett & Ginn. 101: Silver Burdett & Ginn.

Chapter 6 104–105: Eric Carle/Shostal Associates. 106: *l.* Dan De Wilde for Silver Burdett & Ginn; *r.* Imagery. 107: *t., m.* Silver Burdett & Ginn; *b.* Dan De Wilde for Silver Burdett & Ginn. 108: Zimmerman/Alpha. 109: Ken Regan/Camera 5. 110: *t., m.* NASA; *b.* Dan De Wilde for Silver Burdett & Ginn. 111: Dan De Wilde for Silver Burdett & Ginn. 112: Silver Burdett & Ginn. 113: Atoz/Clock, Chicago. 114: Silver Burdett & Ginn. 115: Richard Choy/Peter Arnold, Inc. 116: *b.* Silver Burdett & Ginn. 117: *l.* Silver Burdett & Ginn; *r.* David Lee Guss/Shostal Associates. 118: Dan De Wilde for Silver Burdett & Ginn. 119: *t.* Bill Anderson/Shostal Associates; *b.* Eric Carle/Shostal Associates.

Chapter 7 122–123: Michal Heron. 124: *t., m.* Silver Burdett & Ginn; *b.l.* B. Ullman/Taurus Photos; *b.r.* D.C. Lowe/Shostal Associates. 125: *t.* Dan De Wilde for Silver Burdett & Ginn. 126: *t.l., r.* Dan De Wilde for Silver Burdett & Ginn; *b.l., r.* Silver Burdett & Ginn. 127, 128: Silver Burdett & Ginn. 129: *t.l.* Tom Myers; *t.r.* Silver Burdett & Ginn; *b.* Michal Heron. 130: Silver Burdett & Ginn. 131: Dan De Wilde for Silver Burdett & Ginn. 132–136: Silver Burdett & Ginn. 137: Peter Beck/Alpha. 138: Silver Burdett & Ginn. 139: *l.* © Hank Morgan/Photo Researchers, Inc.; *t.r., b.r.* Ron Mensching/Click, Chicago.

Chapter 8 142–143: E.R. Degginger. 144–145: Silver Burdett & Ginn. 146: Victoria Beller-Smith for Silver Burdett & Ginn. 147: *t.* © Gerry Souter/Photo Researchers, Inc.; *b.l.* E.R. Degginger; *b.r.* © Jim Carter/Photo Researchers, Inc. 148: Dan De Wilde for Silver Burdett & Ginn. 149: *l.* © Hank Morgan/Photo Researchers, Inc.; *r.* Innovative Hearing Corporation. 150: *b.* © Tom McHugh/Photo Researchers, Inc. 151: Silver Burdett & Ginn. 152: *r.* Dan De Wilde for Silver Burdett & Ginn. 153: *t., m.* Frank Siteman/Stock, Boston; *b.* Dan De Wilde for Silver Burdett & Ginn. 155: *t.* David C. Renta/Bruce Coleman; *b.* Rod Planck/Tom Stack & Associates. 156: *b.* © Tom McHugh/Photo Researchers, Inc. 157, 160: Silver Burdett & Ginn. 161: Edison National Historic Site.

Unit Three 164: Frederick D. Bodin/Stock, Boston. 164–165: Robert McKenzie/Tom Stack & Associates. 165: *t.* John Bayalis/Click, Chicago; *b.* E.R. Degginger.

Chapter 9 166–167: Grant Heilman Photography. 169: *l.* © Robert Bornemann/Photo Researchers, Inc.; *r.* Alan Pitcairn/Grant Heilman Photography. 170: Dan De Wilde for Silver Burdett & Ginn. 171: *r.* J.R. Eyerman/Black Star. 172: *l.* © Tom McHugh/Photo Researchers, Inc.; *m.* NASA; *r.* © Wesley Bocxe/Photo Researchers, Inc. 173: *b.* Ken Sakamoto/Black Star. 174, 175: Grant Heilman Photography. 176: Clyde Smith/Peter Arnold, Inc. 177: *l.* © 1987 Nathan Benn/Woodfin Camp & Associates; *r.* Andrew Rakosky/Bruce Coleman. 178: Silver Burdett & Ginn. 179: . Arnold Lann/Black Star; *b.* E.R. Degginger. 180: *t.* Phil Degginger; *b.* © Harald Sund. 181: *l.* Eric Carle/Shostal Associates; *r.* Jeffrey E. Blackman/The Stock Shop. 182: *m., b.* Grant Heilman Photography. 183: C.G. Summers, Jr./Bruce Coleman.

Chapter 10 186–187: E.R. Degginger. 188: *t.* M. Vanderwall/Leo deWys, Inc.; *b.* Warren Dick/Shostal Associates. 189, 190: Silver Burdett & Ginn. 191: *t.* Dick Garvey/West Stock; *b.* Phil Degginger. 192: *t.l.* K.D. Francke/Peter Arnold, Inc.; *m.l.* Breck Kent; *b.l.* Media Vision/Peter Arnold, Inc.; *r.* William Felger/Grant Heilman Photography. 193: *t.* José M. Rosario/Shostal Associates; *b.* © 1987 Longview Daily News 1980 by Roger Werth/Woodfin Camp & Associates. 194: Dan De Wilde for Silver Burdett & Ginn. 195: Jim

Holland/Black Star. 196: *t.* Robert McKenzie/Tom Stack & Associates; *b.* John Colwell/Grant Heilman Photography. 197: *t.l.* © 1987 Martin Rogers/Woodfin Camp & Associates; *t.r.* Laurent Maous/Gamma-Liaison. 197: *b.* Dan De Wilde for Silver Burdett & Ginn. 198: Silver Burdett & Ginn. 199: *l.* Frank Grant/International Stock Photo; *r.* Nick Wheeler/Black Star; *inset* E.R. Degginger. 200: Tom Tracy/The Stock Shop; *inset* E.R. Degginger. 201: *t.l.* © 1987 Michal Heron/Woodfin Camp & Associates; *t.r.* © Paolo Koch/Photo Researchers, Inc.; *b.* Hickson-Bender for Silver Burdett & Ginn.

Chapter 11 204–205: © Tom McHugh/Photo Researchers, Inc. 206: George Rockwin/Bruce Coleman. 207: *b.* E.R. Degginger. 210: Silver Burdett & Ginn. 211: *t.* © Russ Kinne/Photo Researchers, Inc.; *b.* Tom Carroll Photography/Alpha. 212: *t.* Cary Wolinsky/Stock, Boston. 213: *t.* John Curtis/Taurus Photos; *b.* © Lynn Hoffman, Photo Researchers, Inc. 214: *t.l.* Cary Milburn/Tom Stack & Associates; *t.r.* Michael P. Gadonski/Bruce Coleman; *b.* Silver Burdett & Ginn. 215: *t.r.* Douglas Foulke/The Stock Shop; *m.r.* Ron Dillon/Tom Stack & Associates; *b.r.* B. Cory Kilvert, Jr./The Stock Shop. 216: *t.* Cary Wolinsky/Stock, Boston. 217: *t.* Grant Heilman Photography; *m.* John Shaw/Tom Stack & Associates; *b.r.* © Lowell Georgia/Photo Researchers, Inc. 218: Grant Heilman Photography. 220: Silver Burdett & Ginn.

Chapter 12 224–225: NASA. 226: Dan De Wilde for Silver Burdett & Ginn. 227: *m.* E.R. Degginger; *b.* NASA. 228: *l.* Tersch Enterprises; *r.* NASA. 229: *t.* Silver Burdett & Ginn; *b.* NASA. 231: Silver Burdett & Ginn. 232, 233: Tersch Enterprises. 234: Dan De Wilde for Silver Burdett & Ginn. 235: Tersch Enterprises. 236: Silver Burdett & Ginn. 238: Dan De Wilde for Silver Burdett & Ginn. 239: NASA. 242: *t.* Silver Burdett & Ginn; *m.* L.L.T. Rhodes/Taurus Photos; *b.* NASA. 243: © Georg Gerster/Photo Researchers, Inc.

Unit Four 242: *l.* Pat Lanza Field/Bruce Coleman; *r.* David Madison/Duomo. 243: Michal Heron; *inset* Will and Deni McIntyre for Silver Burdett & Ginn.

Chapter 13 248–249: Uselman/H. Armstrong Roberts. 250, 251: Imagery. 252: *t.* Imagery; *b.* Michal Heron. 253: Victoria Beller-Smith for Silver Burdett & Ginn. 254, 255: Copyright by the American Dental Association. Reprinted by permission. 256: Michal Heron. 257: Jeffrey Reed/The Stock Shop. 258: *t.* Porges/Peter Arnold, Inc.; *b.* Silver Burdett & Ginn. 259: John Lei/Stock, Boston. 260: Silver Burdett & Ginn. 261, 263: Dan De Wilde for Silver Burdett & Ginn.

Chapter 14 266–267: Dan De Wilde for Silver Burdett & Ginn. 268: *l.* Dan De Wilde for Silver Burdett & Ginn; *r.* Elizabeth Crewes/Stock, Boston. 269: Silver Burdett & Ginn except *m.l.* © George Leavens/Photo Researchers, Inc. 270: *l.* Focus on Sports; *r.* Silver Burdett & Ginn. 271: *l.* Silver Burdett & Ginn; *t.r.* Jeffrey W. Myers/West Stock; *b.r.* Silver Burdett & Ginn. 272: Walter Chandoha. 273: *l.* Dan De Wilde for Silver Burdett & Ginn; *r.* Silver Burdett & Ginn. 274: Victoria Beller-Smith for Silver Burdett & Ginn. 275: Dan De Wilde for Silver Burdett & Ginn. 276: Martha Cooper. 277: Silver Burdett & Ginn. 278: Victoria Beller-Smith for Silver Burdett & Ginn. 279: Silver Burdett & Ginn. 280: Jacques Jangoux/Peter Arnold, Inc. 281: P. Schuyler/Stock, Boston. 284: *t.* © Stephen Feldman/Photo Researchers, Inc.; *m.* Silver Burdett & Ginn; *b.* Tom Tracy/Medichrome/The Stock Shop. 285: *b.* American Cancer Society.